T0145271

"We Are the Family of a Heroin Addict"

A Real, Raw, and Poignant Story of a Family Through the Recovery of Heroin Addiction

By T. I. Riddick, RN
And Family

"Pikorua", the symbol on the cover was drawn by the daughter of the heroin addict in this book and is the Maori symbol of bonding and growth. It is important to this family as it represents their tie to each other.

Family First!

Preface

Before you start the book, we would like to take this opportunity to thank you for your purchase. We acknowledge that all names have been fictionalized to ensure our ability to publish this and our future books and to alleviate any threat of lawsuit(s). We are a family who live in a small town in the northern part of this great country. We are the epitome of small town America. Everyone knows each other and watches over each other. Our town has a low crime rate and we feel safe here. Heroin addiction has ravaged the fabric of our communities, as in other states across our nation. We are struggling to deal with the fall-out of this "epidemic" and how we, as a family, have been treated, at times, by clinicians and others. We also want to say "thanks" to everyone who has been there for us through this time and for those who were selfless enough to admit that they were also dealing with these addiction issues.

This book idea was born from the hope that if one other family member out in the world could be helped or validated for their emotions and/or thoughts through this time of addiction and recovery, then we have met our goal. We were very tired of people telling us we needed to be something else or feel something else, than what we were feeling at the time. And believe me, all of us have felt different at different times, so you are just getting a snapshot of what we were feeling at the time of the writing. It has been tremendously hard. Frequently we are out of sync with each other. One of us would be furious with her and someone else would understand her plight. We have all loved each other through this and have also "hated" each other at different times. By giving each of our perspectives, we felt we could support other family members and the person with the substance abuse issues.

This book may not be grammatically correct at all time as we are trying to portray our feelings and thoughts which may distort our ability to perfectly write it. Please forgive our errors. Hopefully our journey will carry you through the book. Please feel free to get in touch with us to give us feedback or to get more information from a specific family member online at "We are the family of a heroin addict." or under

T. I. Riddick.

As we got going, we realized there were many people affected by our situation. We decided that this would be the first in a trilogy of books more deeply exploring the relationship addiction has on an entire community.

Again, we would appreciate feedback and would use it in the next book which is titled, "We Are the Extended 'Family' of a Heroin Addict." This is a compilation of the stories of the circle around the family including teachers of the children, police officers in our small town, grandmothers, aunts, uncles, coaches, best friends, and others.

Please feel free to also ask questions or get involved with following our online dialogues as that will help develop the third book in our trilogy, "And I Am the Heroin Addict.", Nicole's Story.

We also hope that clinicians and counselors read these and learn to embrace the journey of the people around the addiction, not just the substance abuser.

Family Forever!

The family in this book is made up of a mother, a father, their two daughters and one son, a son-in law who is the husband of the one of the daughters, and the three children of the oldest daughter who is/ was a heroin addict.

"When the 2ⁿᵈ grade teacher asks, 'What would you like to be when you grow up?' no child ever raises their hand and says, 'I would like to be a crack whore and sell my body to support my need for drugs!' We as a society and clinicians need to look and understand what takes a child from their start to this state of abandonment to their values, beliefs, upbringing and their family."

A Master Trainer of Mental Health Courses

Introduction

We are not trying to save any world but our own, but we did feel isolated in our journey through recovery and are hoping that this book helps others to empathize with their own journey. Each family member wrote their own chapter, with me helping the young boys to document theirs. We have not censored our perceptions. It is real. You might want more or less from one of our family members but this is about healing and not opening up all the wounds that are here in us. No one was asked to cut or put more in than they were comfortable writing down. Having said that, we did censor ourselves. The last chapter, Nicole's, is done at three distinct times and we wanted to keep that so people could read the chaos of her being high, the sadness of getting sober and the joy of her freedom. Our son's chapter is fairly limited as he has been away from the day to day struggles of her recovery. That is fine with us, and it shows how conflicted he was because he loved her for caring for him when he was young and then hated her for how she didn't care for her children and now tolerates her and is learning how to be back in relationship with her. It is hard to read our other daughter's chapter as she has been the most burdened by the experience. Being "the responsible child" has fatigued her at times. These are all valid perspectives. The chapters written by Nicole's children were very hard, as well. They have experienced more than they ever should have been exposed to in their young lives. It was our daughter's greatest wish that her name be the only one left whole as it is part of her recovery to own all she has done, caused and created; good and bad.

We are also trying to help substance abuse counselors and clinicians to not recreate in their treatment the self-centeredness inherent in the person with the addiction. The supports for Nicole allowed her to be focused on herself and only herself for 18 months. Our family was fortunate enough to be able to support, both financially and emotionally, her children while she was getting sober and learning to live sober. There was nowhere she could do that with her children safely. It has uncovered for us a huge failing of the system of supports in treating addiction. We also want counselors to stop blaming the families for the addict's use. It was tiring for Nicole to constantly have to defend us and it made her leave providers who may have helped her. At one point, she actually asked me, "Did something happen to me in my childhood that you didn't tell me?" What does causing her to doubt her perception of her great childhood, being very loved and cared for, do to help her own her responsibility for having started using illicit substances?

The editorial staff asked if one of the reasons for writing this book was to help us heal as a family. We all can adamantly say,"NO!" to that question. It was painful and we all have cried numerous times reading, fixing, adding details, rereading, etc. our and each other's chapters. What is healing our family and changing our pain into joy is our daughter's journey of recovery and the "living amends" she does every day with us. She tries to live remorse, not be remorseful, by being the person she was called and raised to be with her children and the rest of us. She still screws it up but now quickly recognizes it and makes amends. WE are a family that loves each other and we work every day to be strong together.

We are the family of a heroin addict.

Family Forever!

Chapter 1

"I am the mother of a heroin addict."

Many people write about events that "…changed their life…" Often, I have been surprised about what those events have been for these individuals. They will say meeting their future spouse/significant other changed their life or having their first child changed their life. For me that was not the case. My life was on a trajectory that I planned from early childhood. I had love in my life, so I knew I would love and therefore I would find someone that I could commit to and live with for the rest of my life. I knew we would have children, so those events, as blessed as they were, again were a part of the projected expectations I had for myself and my life's path.

Truly, the event that changed my life was the call I received on April 19th, 2016, from my husband. He asked where I was so I told him, and he said, "You need to get to my mother's house, Nicole took more money and has just admitted to me that she is a heroin addict." I know he said other things and I tried to listen, but after those words,"…she is a heroin addict." I stopped thinking, hearing, feeling, processing. My life changed in that instant. I no longer was a good mother. I no longer had raised my daughter right. I no longer existed on a plane of life where addiction to heroin was in someone else's family, not mine. I no longer could have that arrogance that something must have made that person need to use heroin to get through their day. I no longer had a daughter on whom I could depend. I didn't even know my daughter. How could she be a heroin addict? I now know this was a part of who she is, was and would continue to be for a period of time, after. I no longer was a competent psych nurse. I had worked with the substance abuse population; how could I deny what was right there in front of my face. My life was irrevocably changed in that instance. It continued to change over the next 18 months, up to the date that I write my chapter.

When I arrived at my mother-in-law's home, I walked into total silence. Four people sitting in the living room. I looked at them all, my husband rigidly furious and hurt, my mother-in-law teary and weeping, my younger sister-in-law stoically trying to hold it together and my daughter, with tears streaming down her face. All eyes on me. Now what? I asked Nicole, "Is it true? Are you addicted to heroin?" and she simply said, "Yes, mom." I remember shaking my head, saying, "Ok." I then looked to my husband and said, "She will be admitted to the psych/substance abuse unit, detox must start to happen immediately. We need to take care of her three children while that is going on and we need a family meeting to determine any glitches anyone can find. Please call the other kids and notify them that we rally all together, so this can be dealt with and done and over. And all of this needs to be done in the next 38 hours because I am leaving on my planned trip with the 4 oldest grandchildren to go 12 hours south so they can see their uncle at college and watch him play in a lacrosse game." They all looked at me, said ok, and it happened. She also gave me Power of Attorney over her 3 kids which allowed me to get some things done that needed to get done. The flaw to this great and glorious plan is that I took control, became the nurse instead of the mom, denied all my devastation and just kept on getting things done. Nicole was admitted the day I left with the kids to go to their uncle's game and everyone thought we were now on our way to regaining control over this situation.

I hear you all laughing or shaking your head at our naiveté, but that is what we thought at that time. We had a plan, we followed it and so it should be good. We got to New York and the call came in from her that she was fully admitted to the unit and she was really scared. I told her to be brave for her kids, her family and everything she holds good in this life. She made it through day 1 into day 2, but by day 3, I got a call from her that they had discharged her because they had helped her detox and she was on her way to getting better. This was a lie-she left on her own.

I believed her. I believed her that she was clean when she couldn't get her kids to school on time, when she couldn't be woken up to get to her son's medical appointment. And I believed that she was still clean when more money was taken from my husband and me. I believed her, even when my other daughter, called me and said that there was expensive personal property that was missing after Nicole had been there to help watch over her nephews (2) and niece. I still believed in her when checks were taken out of the checkbook and written for large amounts of money at a large chain store, only to have large ticket items returned to get the cash back. I could go on and on. Over the next three months there was much I denied because I believed in her, the medical field that said they had helped her, and her love for her kids.

I stopped believing in August 23rd, 2016, when her middle child rode his bike out into the road and was hit by a car. Nicole couldn't be found because she was upstairs in her apartment sleeping off using heroin. He was 6 years old. His 5 year old little brother watched it all. Her 14 year old daughter thought she knew where Nicole was and ran up the stairs to get her up. They rushed him to the hospital where he was found to be just bruised, nothing broken. That was the beginning of the end of my denial, stupidity and tolerance for her being a complete bonehead.

After that incident, she made promises, she cleaned up her apartment, she told the kids things would change, she got a great job at the local state psych hospital. She was very good at her job, so much so, she got promoted before she got out of orientation. Five weeks after her son was hit by a car, on October 1, 2016, she was arrested at her apartment for criminal behavior on state grounds. Her children were not present at the apartment when she was arrested. Her daughter, however, was texted by all her friends about what was going on at her house. Three police cars surrounded my mother-in-law's home, where Nicole and her children lived at the time. I moved her 3 children into our home and they have lived with us for over a year, at this writing.

The early years

Nicole, my first daughter, was such a lovely, sweet, warm child. She was responsible, outgoing and loved by all the many members of our extended family. She never acted spoiled, but she once told me that being so well loved, she didn't know evil existed. I asked for more clarity and she said she had been unprepared that there were people in the world who would not be good to and for her. I have thought about that statement many times over the last 18 months. She said this after she had moved out of our home and had been living in her own place with a significant other, for about 5 years. She was 24 years old. I will leave this part of the story to her chapter, but I will say that she experienced events outside of her repertoire of coping strategies and understanding. Maybe her upbringing had not helped her develop the mental toughness she needed to deal with certain difficult situations?

Nicole was a beautiful caregiver to her younger siblings. She is 5 years older than her sister and 12 years older than her brother. My mother would say when she came to visit she had to fight to get near our son because Nicole, ("the little mother"), would not let her too close. She was so helpful and was by far the easiest for my husband to work with and/or leave a list of things to get done. She always took huge pride in her spot in our family and would brag it up in her school journals or to her grandparents. My husband and I did not drink or use substances, so it wasn't a part of our family culture. Though after I write that statement I remember my husband smoking cigarettes early on but he still did not do it in front of any of our kids and it has been over 20 years since he stopped. I vaguely remember him smoking a little in the living room when his parents or siblings came to visit because almost all of them smoked cigarettes, too. But again Nicole has validated that we did not use any substance in front of her so it wasn't environmental that triggered her use. So what did???? As a parent I want to see the bigger picture. As a nurse I want to know how to help her and I want to help others not to choose to use heroin the first time.

She herself did not use substances in her high school years, but she did get pregnant with my granddaughter and delivered her in the fall of her senior year. That was a huge event in our family because again, I thought we had done everything right. There was no shaming associated with normal desires and adolescent behavior. We had set up other adults she could talk to if she didn't feel comfortable talking to us about birth control. She did things correctly to protect herself, but she is just one of those people for whom oral contraceptives don't work as well to prevent pregnancy. Two of her three children were conceived despite oral birth control. She was loving and caring and decided she wanted her child. We all did. Parenthood began for her at the early age of 17, which she does admit had a huge impact on her. But she is clear; it was not a causal circumstance for her use of heroin. So what did create the circumstances where she said yes the first time to using an illicit substance? I was very ready to read her chapter, the last chapter of our book as a family, to see if she was ever able to articulate the turning point or was it a series of turning points?

Back to Now

While she has been recovering, my husband and I have had her three children. For over a year now, we have had her children. This was neither our journey, nor our hope for our future. We had one year and 5 weeks after our son went away to college to be empty nesters-HA!!! We had diminished our responsibilities after he left. It was just the two of us. If one of us wanted to eat and the other didn't, there was no stress. If we wanted to eat out, we did. Our grocery bill went down to the point we could buy filet mignon and not worry about the cost because it was just the two of us and we saved grocery money everywhere else. We were learning to just be a couple, without children actively needing our care and attendance.

When the children came to us, they were a 14-year-old girl (freshman), a 6-year-old boy (1st grader) and a 5-year-old boy (Kindergartner). The father of my granddaughter is an addict, too, and has provided little to the financial and emotional well-being of his daughter. In fact, he probably has done his fair share of damage to her. She clearly does not believe he will follow through with anything he says to her. An example of this is when he promised that for her 2016 birthday and 2016 Christmas presents, he would pay for her driver's education. This was huge to her because she knew that driving was tied to her and her brothers' independence and safety (she talks about this in her chapter). She was cautiously optimistic because he had a steady job doing meat cutting at a national grocery chain and had been paying a small amount of child support. He came through and paid the first down payment for the classes. She started classes but not long after, the instructor asked her if her father was making the next agreed upon payment to the driving school. She came to me, distraught and so embarrassed again by a parent, realizing that she was not going to be able to finish. When she got ahold of him, he told her he had lost his job because he had gotten drunk and had overslept so, he wasn't going to be able to finish paying. She contacted his mother, brother, and sister to ask if they could help pay for it. She begged for anything from them. She would have been happy for ten bucks from any one of them. But no, they did not help her. Our family, a great-aunt, Nana T. (76), her uncle & his girlfriend (both college students), her aunt and uncle, and her mother, Nicole (now 7 months clean & sober) and my husband & I came up with the $275.00 left over. She has her permit and is driving. Ironically, she can't drive with either of her parents as neither have driver's licenses. She has lost the belief that her father can ever help her.

My grandsons' father is in prison for theft due to his need for drugs. Again, even in our small world we see the reality of the epidemic of substance abuse and addiction. He has been in jail/prison for over half of the life of his youngest child. He parents (the other grandparents) are in denial and will say what a good father he is to his boys. I don't understand. He was my daughter's dealer. He has contributed little to nothing for child support (financially or emotionally), and he has been in prison for 2.5 years (non-consecutively) for the last five years with another year and three months to go. One of our friends, who is a local police officer said, "He is doing life on the installment plan." It is horrifying that he will continue to go in and out of prison over the course of these two little boy's lives. The hardest thing I have had to do in caring for the two boys is to allow them to go to prison to see their dad with the other grandparents. Again, nothing I asked for in my life.

When the children moved in with my husband and me, they had many things that needed modification. My granddaughter had been thrust into the parent role so much; she did not know ordinary boundaries in caring for her brothers. I was constantly stating to her, "K., I'm right here. Let me deal with the boys' behavior." She also didn't trust we would be home at the time we said we would. When we knew she was sad or angry her emotional responses weren't normal. She would have an almost flat, emotional response. We saw it as a tremendous breakthrough when she cried, hard, over a distressing event. Finally, she had stopped putting up the block between events in her life and her emotions. That took a solid six months.

The boys had no routine to their lives and needed a lot of guidance around basic care like brushing teeth, bathing, smelling good, matching clothes, eating in a social way. None of these things were too significant on their own, but seeing the whole package convinced us something was not right. They were significantly obese as well. The older boy frequently refused to eat unprocessed food. We found out later, at his first dental exam, the reason for that. He had nine teeth with cavities in them. He had to go under anesthesia to get his teeth fixed. My husband stayed during the procedure. He said it was one of the most horrific events he had to witness. The doctor only put him under light sedation and A. was writhing in pain. My husband told me this after we had driven away from the office and A. had dozed off. His eyes were full of tears and he railed at the fact that our daughter had been so selfish in her addiction that she would never know the pain A. went through. My husband said he would never forgive her for not taking better care of the precious gift of her child. That night A. looked at my husband and said, "Pappy, this is the first time I can remember eating without having any pain in my teeth. This was a great day." My husband smiled and said, "That is great buddy, this is a good day." But that night we both cried and wondered where we went wrong with Nicole. How could this happen?

I mentioned the boys' obesity. The boys ate more food than they should have, and not good quality food. Since coming to live with us, the oldest has lost 29 pounds and the youngest has lost 26 pounds. Please remember, they are only 6 & 7 years old. Both boys had a physical exam right before coming to live with me. Both at times in this past year they have needed to see the family practitioner for minor problems, like a sore throat. The doctors have been amazed at their weight loss but also their overall physical health and asked what happened. I just told them it is good food and lots of exercise. The boys had no idea of portions; they would eat 2-3 packages of breakfast toaster pastries a day. That means they were eating up to 1260 calories just in that food, let alone everything else they ate that day. In the boys section, they talk a lot about loving their bodies now and their physical abilities. Both have always been very athletic, now even more so, and they love it. Again, how did I not know something was wrong? Why didn't I interact earlier? Why did I listen to my daughter when she said that it was just part of their genes, that she and their dad are bigger people? Why? Why? Why? Over and over, I blame myself for not being more aggressive in looking at the finer details.

This entire situation has taken tremendous amount of money. Money we had secured for our retirement. It has strained our marriage to its breaking point, at least three times. This threat to our 33 year marriage is one of the things that will be the hardest to forgive when Nicole reintegrates into our lives. The cracks of our marriage have become breaks. It is hard to be parenting young children, an adolescent girl and be a couple of 54 year olds who are really the grandparents. We have been thrust into the role of parents. Everyone tells us that we are doing the right thing and we do not believe differently. It is the right thing to do, though it does not make this any easier to get through this day, this moment.

I also have struggled with my own mental health/substance abuse colleagues who keep saying that I need to understand that Nicole needs time to get into her sobriety, recover, figure out how she lives clean. They say that I really shouldn't let my anger show so much because it stresses her out and this could lead to a relapse. Really???? I should cover up my emotions when she calls me a "C_NT!", because she got some paranoid thought that I had driven the 45 minutes down to the city she was living in, for some other reason than to get her to sign a piece of paper and call a case manager in front of me to decrease her legal problems. I should forgive her when her child is writhing in pain because she didn't take care of him. I should not be upset that her daughter has to cover all her emotions. Really??? I had a colleague of mine say, "Use some Motivational Interviewing techniques with her, which should help." OMG!! She's my daughter, not my client, you freakin' wombat!!!

I also don't appreciate the counselors consistently stating that something must have happened in Nicole's childhood to create her need for the substances. She has told them constantly that she had a great childhood, full of love, encouragement, belief that she could do anything she wants, etc. but they want her to think on it and get back to them on what she feels the abuses are from childhood that led her to this place. At this point, she does look at her childhood differently but for what benefit. She was never abused, she was loved. What benefit is it to put that into question? Look to her abusive adult relationship with the boys' dad because that is where it started and stop putting the blame on us.

Not enough is done about the circle that surrounds the addict. The treatment model has swung so far that it has almost become a very self-indulgent reflection of the addiction itself. Addiction by nature is a self-indulgent, selfish, self-centered process. Let's not recreate that in the care of the addict. There are no true sober houses for parents with children in our state. So our daughter has been learning to be sober without the major stressors of her life alongside of her sobriety. How's that going to work when she gets the boys back overnight. One day without them and the next with the day to day grind and joy of being a full time single parent. Her daughter has chosen to stay with my husband and me, so she can finish her high school at the school she started so Nicole has lost that, but she will still have a 6 & 7 year old set of boys that need constant support. And she needs to stay sober.

As I end my chapter, I think of all that has happened and I try to be gentle on myself. I try to remind myself that I have the right to my emotions and any screwy way I feel. I try to be gentle on others in our family, too, about how they feel. I am not always perfect at it and I screw up plenty, but I always try and I pray a lot of the time, to just help me through. I dream of the future when Nicole is back; close to me. It has been wonderful to watch her get back to the person I knew her as before this dark time came to pass. I pray that when my grandsons go back to her, they will stay safe and she will see the joy they are in this world. I also pray that the damage done will make them stronger, not vulnerable, to their future. Overall, I just pray, hope and dream! May that be enough.

I am the mother of a heroin addict and I hate that. I hate everything about that. I hold the hope that there will be a day that is not the first thought I have, or that it will be a thought of I **was** the mother of a heroin addict, but now I am again just a mother.

Chapter 2

"I am the father of a heroin addict."

When we bring a child into this world we have no idea what we are facing. We do our best based on how we were raised and what we saw of the way others raised their kids. But when your kid is in their thirties and decides to finally let you in on a dirty little secret that they are a drug addict, everything you tried to build on goes right out the window.

You believe, in some part of your mind, that you will be there for them through the time you have here with them. And I have been with our drug addict daughter. I tried to help raise her to be respectful and understand right from wrong. We provided every possible opportunity for her to excel in any endeavor that she decided she wanted to pursue as she grew up. I have been her financial stability, as needed. I have loved her children, even if I have hated the circumstances in which they were born. In short, I have done my best to guide her through some very difficult decisions her entire life. Being my first child, she was a life changing event for me. I have always tried to make a priority of providing what was needed by her.

Now, life is a totally different set of circumstances. She became a heroin addict. The single mother of three children, by two different men. Both are non-providers, for her, or any of the kids. After years of trying to help guide her through difficult choices, I was made absolutely powerless for her, by her.

She was always the young girl that was attracted to the wrong kind of guys. It was extremely difficult to see the choices she made. Getting pregnant her senior year was devastating to me. She had the whole world in front of her and decided to hang out with the wrong person. Her child is a beautiful young lady. Now 15 years old, with exposure to more than most people will ever have to see in their lifetime. All due to her mother's CHOICES. The other two children are six and seven year old boys. As of this writing, they have been living with us for eleven months. All are thriving and have learned what it is to have as normal a life as we can provide.

We have been through hell as far as dealing with her issues. We have done everything we could in trying to deal with her CHOICES.

Years ago things started going downhill when she started hanging out with the boys' father. She was living down the road from our house, so everything was kind of in our face. I would drive by, going to and coming from work, and see their yard looking worse and worse. Our daughter and the boys' dad started to look trashier as well. They only be worked sporadically, and they started becoming a financial drain on us. We would not let the grandkids go without being able to have things they needed and take part in activities they deserved to be in.

As things progressed we moved her and the three children into my mother's apartment. My dad had passed and the apartment was right on the second floor of my parent's house. This arrangement was supposed to afford our daughter and kids a safe place to live and provide oversight for my mother in her times of need, as well. At this point the boy's father was already heading down his own path of self-destruction and no longer a permanent fixture in their lives.

The decline was obvious, in retrospect. Items were starting to disappear, checks were being taken and maintaining a job was becoming impossible.

Issues started coming faster and faster as things spiraled down. She continued to hang around the wrong people. She allowed other people to start staying on, for short durations, in the apartment. None of these people were welcome there, in my eyes, as we were paying the rent, and other extras, for her to live there. I stopped by one weekday, to check on how things were going. Nine thirty in the morning and it appeared everyone was still in bed. I banged on the door until my granddaughter answered the door. When I asked where her mother was, I was told she was still in bed. And she was, with the father of the boys. At this time there had already been an order of protection prohibiting him from being in their lives. Neither of them were working at the time and the kids were getting no direction in their lives from either one of their parents.

We attended Youth Night for the kid's football teams. An evening where the boys would be able to run onto the high school field as part of the half-time celebration. An evening that should have been nothing but pride for me, seeing third generation football players being recognized. As I was leaving, part way through the second half, one of the local police sergeants stopped me and asked if I was aware of what had happened at the apartment the previous Thursday night. My heart sank and he could see I was not informed.

On that Thursday evening, two of my daughter's friends went to the apartment at about nine o'clock, a school night. The couple ended up going in the bathroom and she gave him a strong enough heroin injection that he required naloxone to save his life. There were ambulance and police at the apartment for this event, which my granddaughter had witnessed. She was thirteen.

These events are but a very few that we have had to live. We have experienced thoughts and feelings that I didn't even know existed. To actually sit in the evening and discuss with my wife that we need to be prepared for the police to show up and tell us our daughter is dead, to the worries of the grandkids. I actually took our daughter in to the police station once because she had an arrest warrant out for her. I cried like a baby as the police processed her for arrest.

The feelings start out as "What the hell is she thinking?" to "Where did WE go wrong?" In the end I have become very distant….from her. We currently have the three children living with us, the best thing for them. But, this is a circumstance that is extremely unnatural for us. Our youngest, a son, is attending college with a huge package based on his academic and lacrosse proficiencies. Our other daughter is married with three kids, living on her own, with a fantastic husband. We are supposed to be "empty nesters." We actually experienced "freedom" until eleven months ago, when we decided we needed to take in the grandkids. Our daughter had been arrested, again. Even when you know what you're doing is the right thing it has been extremely trying on us. The financial hemorrhaging that we are experiencing has put our retirement plans in jeopardy. We have been dealing with all the needs of the kids for several years. We have purchased three vehicles over this time. We have paid all the rent, as well as most other living expenses for our oldest daughter. Tens of thousands of dollars are simply gone. Our daughter is holding us hostage with the grandkids because we couldn't let them go without.

I hate what has happened from the CHOICES that my daughter has made. It has fragmented what was once a very strong family. We have done all we could, time after time, trying to influence her and help her get her act back together. Every time we tried, she continued on the same path.

Once we had the kids with us, I attempted to monitor what our daughter was posting on social media. One of the grandsons had to have an operation. One our daughter failed to make sure was done when she had him. She posted when he was out of surgery on social media. A private medical procedure was now made open to the world. When I said something about the posting, she blocked me. That has been the end of any communication between us. She has texted me, but I have nothing to say to her anymore. My wife has seen medical, dental and eye issues were taken care of in the eleven months that we have had the kids. Issues that should have been taken care of years ago, but were not. When a seven year old can lose 28 plus or minus pounds and a six year old loses 25 plus or minus pounds, they were simply not being properly cared for; they were abused. By simply having them on a regular bed time and eating the right food they have made huge strides in their lives. They realize their clothes now don't stink and they care about the way they dress and present themselves. It is amazing what simply caring about a child can do for them.

This is all because of CHOICES. It really disgusts me when addiction is referred to as a disease. It has been my EXPERIENCE that the addict is the disease to everyone around them. Our daughter has been like a cancer, destroying young kids hope and pride, as well as everyone else around her.

There was a time that I felt responsible for what she CHOSE to do. Now I realize SHE is the only one to blame. We have had way too many sleepless nights wondering what would happen next. We went through the whole "why" phase of this mess. We have made so many attempts at trying to get her to change with her simply denying where she was. We have sacrificed our bank accounts to the extreme and our future isn't clear for us anymore.

The parenting differences between a mother and father need to be discussed as well. As her father I have attempted to GIVE direction. It is what fathers do, I believe. I have tried to handle my emotions when alone. Tried to be the strong, well-grounded voice of reason. It has killed a part of me. I have great difficulty with compassion. I have great difficulty with trusting people around me. And I have formed a very strong sense of just what this "epidemic" really is. These differences have caused a great deal of difficulty in maintaining my marriage. My wife works in mental health. She has strong beliefs. She tends to be much more trusting and understanding than I do. She has made an absolute priority of the grandchildren. Yes, I believe the kids need to be *a* priority. But my advice to anyone who has to endure anything like what we have, would be to remember that your marriage needs to remain a top priority as well.

These last months we have been invaded. Do not get me wrong, I absolutely love my grandchildren. By having to be the primary disciplinarian in a grandchild's life has absolutely diminished my ability to simply have joy in having them around. It is a very unnatural role to suddenly be thrust back to having young children that you are absolutely responsible for. At first there was an extremely deep fear. I already fucked up their mother's life what am I going to do with them? Not an easy hurdle when you're now the person kissing them goodnight and seeing them to bed. The simple things that we had started to enjoy, going to the bathroom in my underwear, now became inappropriate. Having time with my wife in the evening, gone. Simply coming and going in our own house as we pleased was now a thing of the past.

I am well beyond blaming myself anymore. Our daughter was in her late twenties when all this started to rain down over our ENTIRE FAMILY'S lives. The things that they do to get money to support their CHOICES goes well beyond normal comprehension. Our daughter stole from her own family. There are items missing that will always be the responsibility of her CHOICES. She wrote a bad check on an account with my deceased father's name on it. I will NEVER get beyond that one. We ran behind her cleaning up her deceptions, all on our own dime. We felt responsible, she is our daughter, after all. This is a relatively small town we live in. We are known by most folks in the area. It has been difficult to continually face friends and neighbors knowing that some of them have been affected by all this.

There is a ripple effect that doesn't get any recognition with this whole "EPIDEMIC". When our daughter and/or her boyfriend were out taking tools from local contractors it made it difficult for them to feed their families. It made delays in work being completed on homes that people needed to move into. They wasted the time and resources of law enforcement. There ARE more important things for everyone to be doing rather than dealing with the poor CHOICES of an addict. The long term effects on the kids is still to be seen. How would you feel if you were six, seven or fifteen years old and your mother failed to maintain custody of you because of her CHOICES, and your father was in prison? I can't even imagine the pain these kids feel. They have now had a completely safe environment with proper diet and all needs met, for months. They have responded absolutely, unbelievably, well. Their respect is through the roof, their pride is enormous and the love they show is undeniable.

I want to be clear that there MAY be circumstances where someone becomes an addict through prescription drugs. Once the addiction is recognized there is an absolute need to make correction. We pursued our daughter, asking her to get help, for a long period of time. Her refusal to be honest with herself, at the sacrifice of her children and family, is purely selfish. Denial is a weakness, not a DISEASE.

The financial cost of what we have endured is mind boggling. I would never wish our experience on anyone. I feel very lucky we had the resources because many others would have had to let their grandchildren go into foster care to be cared for. As I have said, not only have we spent the best part of our bank accounts on trying to help her with this, we have also put our marriage on the brink of failure. I have been married to my wife for thirty-three years. Our daughter's CHOICES have been significant enough to push us to the brink of failing. That is just the first ripple we have felt. If we fail, what message would that send to our other kids, our grandkids and others? In the end, we WILL make the CHOICES to ensure our love survives this.

I will speak of only our experience when I say it has been something that I could not have imagined dealing with. I would not wish this on my worst enemy. And it ALL started with the CHOICES of one individual. That individual has been living with only her own needs to meet, for the past eleven months. I have several questions that come to mind. Did she ever really want the kids to begin with? If so, why weren't they put first? Will she relapse? There is an extremely high probability that could happen. Has she damaged herself with this abuse that she isn't able to make proper decisions for her kids? The introduction of chemicals that you have no idea where they came from, into your body certainly can have irreversible effects. Will any of the kids end up taking the journey their parents did? They are all old enough to realize, if nothing else, where their parents are.

I do not know the answers to put a stop to the CHOICES that people are making. I do believe that the prescription drugs NEED to be looked at. Another thing is the elimination of those who CHOOSE to make a business out of the illicit drugs. NOT providing the naloxone safety net. That sounds cold, but when there is actual political conversation about providing "safe houses" with medical attendees for the use of these drugs we have failed as a society.

I hope that we see a resurgence in FAMILY VALUES. We may be going broke, but we have provided for our grandchildren where their parents CHOSE not to. If their parents had the same priorities I wouldn't be writing this, more importantly our grandkids would be in a safe home with TWO loving parents.

My darkest moment in life will be when they are returned back to their mother, the one who CHOSE to create this issue to begin with. One father that has never supported his daughter and the other in prison for over another year. He will have been in prison over half of the boys lives. My heart breaks just putting that to paper.

I am the father of a heroin addict and I hate what my daughter has done to our family, especially to her children, and my wife and me.

Chapter 3

"I am the sister of a heroin addict."

I hate the way that sounds, and I hate how rough it is coming out of my mouth. If you speak to me in person, I will just refer to her as my "crackhead sister" because it's easier than explaining the truth behind my side of the story. My sister was supposed to be my person, my best friend, my support system through my struggles. Instead, throughout the years, I have had to protect my heart and my truth for fear of upsetting her. Instead of having a sister to exchange kids for the weekend with, I have a sister who will never again be allowed to be alone with my children. I have a husband who has told me "If it were up to me, she would never be in our lives again" and I have three kids who may never have a positive relationship with their aunt. Heroin is affecting an alarming number of families throughout our country, and for that, I am willing to share my side of the story, in hopes that just one person gains from it.

A little information about me: I have three beautiful babies (7 years old, 4 years old, and 2 years old) and an amazing husband who has supported me through every step of this chaos. I work in the mental health field and do have some experience with substance abuse in my professional life. This does not make it any easier to deal with a family member who is an addict. I have spent a lot of time over the last 18 months struggling to manage my emotions around my sister, which swing from anger to pride for her sobriety, sympathy to full hatred and from supportive to fuck off. If you are the sister of a drug addict, don't let anyone tell you how to feel about the situation. You are allowed to feel how you feel. This has taken me a long time to come to terms with.

Your wedding is supposed to be the best day of your life, surrounded by love and family and friends. I was pregnant with my second child throughout the planning process of the wedding. I remember being so frustrated with my sister. She was my maid of honor; she was supposed to be helping me with the planning, the list making, and the decorations. I didn't have that. I was lucky enough to have a mother, a mother-in-law, and stepmother-in-law who were an amazing support to me throughout this process. They planned my wedding shower, helped me organize my plans, and helped with last minute details. I never got a bachelorette party or a night with my wedding party because it was just never organized. It was annoying, but I was pregnant and couldn't do much anyway, so did it really matter? At the time I was upset about it, but it is what it is, right? My bridesmaids were either pregnant with me, or under the age of 18 so it wasn't a huge deal.

On my wedding day, I remember my sister telling me that she "has taken something" to help calm her nerves. I didn't really react because I was busy worrying about the wedding and everything going on around me. Looking back on that day is hard. I have come to realize that my sister was high at my wedding. How do you forgive someone for that? How do you move past knowing that she was not able to make a speech that made sense because getting high was more important than her little sister's wedding? This has forever been something that I have held onto. There have been conversations about it but I don't think my sister has realized how hard it is to look back on and know that she may not remember most of that day.

Over the next three years, I watched my sister spiral out of control. I became a stay at home mom of my two children and watched my two nephews as well. She would pick them up late and argue with me if I called her to find out where she was. She would constantly ask for money, even when she knew that I didn't have any. I am, admittedly, a people pleaser and have a very hard time saying no. I usually found a way to try and help her get money, be it with returnables or change. I watched, as she would make plans to come spend time with the kids and I but have her never show up, or spend most of her time on the phone. Usually, an extended time on the phone was followed by an "I'm going to run to the store for a soda" and her not returning for an hour or so.

In the last five years, I have struggled to maintain my relationship with my sister. From her telling me that she was using while at my wedding, to her not answering her phone the day my youngest son was born because of her drug addiction, to having personal items taken from my home after she had been there, never to be found again. I have tried to be there for my sister. I believed her when she told me that she was "only using enough to feel normal" on the few occasions that she was honest with me. I believed her when she told me that she was clean after her first attempt at getting clean (I use "attempt" loosely as she left the hospital less than 72 hours after being admitted and used on her way home). I was the person who spent two hours searching her apartment after this first "attempt" to try and make her home a safe place for her to come home to, throwing away an entire box of shit that may or may not have been related to her drug use. I don't think I will ever get over that day. The straight fear of having her get out of the hospital was terrible. I've spent months of being in fear every time my phone rang, worried that this was the call telling me that she had overdosed. Even when you hate the person an addict has become, you love them regardless, and knowing that at any moment you may get a call saying that they are dead is terrifying.

My parents decided to remove my niece and nephews from my sister about 7 months ago, after a particularly bad time with my sister's addiction. We were at a football game for the oldest three boys (my oldest child and my two nephews), and we all could tell that something was off with my sister. She was wearing sunglasses even though it was overcast and almost raining. She could barely hold a conversation, and she refused to take her sunglasses off. I would later find out that she had spent the weekend on a bender, using cocaine and heroin, and had barely slept. This was followed by police coming to my sister's apartment to search the apartment, along with charges related to theft from a new job that she had obtained. About a week after my parent's taking the kids, I had them for the weekend, and it happened to be my sister's birthday. I made a cake with her kids, and brought it to the football field to let them celebrate with her, but she was too selfish to even get the strain it was putting on us.

There were times that she took the kids on her own, but they were few and far between because each time she did, something would happen. One weekend that they were staying with me because my parents went to see my brother play fall lacrosse at his college, there was a family day in our town. We decided that all the kids would enjoy it, and that she should come too. We were trying to maintain some amount of "normal" for her kids while things were in chaos. She took the kids to walk to the park and was supposed to meet us there by a specific time. She ended up being 1.5 hours later than she was supposed to be. My niece told me once we got back to my house that they had "gone to some sketchy house about 20 minutes away and she left us in the car the entire time." This was the last time I was willing to be the person responsible for her having the children alone. She never had her kids alone again. It was just upsetting that she didn't get that it was wrong to drag her kids to these dangerous places.

I think that is one of the hardest things for me to understand. My sister put her addiction above everything else throughout the last few years. She didn't care who she hurt, or how bad the damage was. I hated her for a long time for the shit she brought into our lives. She caused family fights, issues with my husband and me, and put my children in danger the few times I had her watch them. She took several things from me and my family. She let strange people in my house when I wasn't home. She has admitted to a few things here and there, but the hard thing is that I have a feeling she took more than I even realize, be it money or jewelry that has gone missing. What she doesn't realize is that she caused lasting problems within our family unit. There are bridges that may never be rebuilt.

I was the person who took my sister to detox when she was finally "ready" to be clean. I was called at work and asked to leave to bring her to a town 45 minutes away to go to a program that would allow her to detox around addiction resources, rather than in our small town with no support. I dreaded being in the car with her. I did that drive for my mom, not my sister. At this point, I didn't care if she lived or died. In my mind, our lives would have been so much easier if she had just died. There wouldn't be fear, there wouldn't be the worry that she would just go right back to her ways. Now, if you are reading this and you don't have an addict in your life you may not understand how a sister can say that, but I honestly hated her. I was dead convinced that this drive would be the last time that I would see my sister. I didn't believe that she would survive detox, and I also believed that even if she did, that she would be using again within 24 hours after discharge. We stopped at a gas station near the detox center to grab something to drink and use the restroom. I would find out later that she had heroin on her and that she used in the bathroom right before I dropped her off.

Throughout the drive, I remember telling her that she needed to admit some of her wrong doings and that she needed to get better or she was never going to have her family back. She admitted a few things to me, like that she had taken my husband's bow from our closet and pawned it, but that she had no clue where mine (which was in the same closet, right next to my husband's) had gone. I know that she most likely had something to do with my missing bow, but to date, I have not gotten confirmation on this. I never pressed charges on her for anything. My husband would have done differently, but he understands that this is my sister, regardless of the shitty things she has done. I cried for a while after dropping her off, again under the impression that there was a good chance that it was the last time that I would see her. I finally was able to pull myself together enough to call my dad and let him know where my sister had pawned my husband's bow, and he was able to get it back, which I am very grateful for.

I guess the reason that I added that part into the story was to point out how forgiving you can be even when you hate someone. I very easily could have pressed charges on my sister for several different things, but I chose not to. I couldn't do that to my niece and nephews, but I also wanted to make sure that, if she was able to get her life back together, she was not forever followed by her mistakes. People deserve second chances, most of the time. It does get harder every time, but I'm a big believer in trying to accept people for who they are, good and bad.

While my parents are the ones who have taken my sister's three kids, my husband and I spend a lot of time with the kids. I watch them every day after school, and I have them on weekends if my parents are taking a trip, or sometimes just to give my parents a break. It has spun my house upside down, as well. On any given day I have 5 kids, ages 2-7, at my house, while my sister is living her life, 45 minutes away, with no responsibilities. I think that this is one of the hardest parts for me. While she is sober, and I am proud of her for that, my life can be in chaos at times because of her sobriety. At this point in time, I thought that my sister and I would be trading weekends with our kids so we could take a break from the crazy, but instead I am helping my parents raise her kids, while she is enjoying spending time at the beach or spending time with friends. The most recent frustration was Easter. I had her children, as well as my own, and made sure that all kids had things for Easter morning. That same weekend, my sister got a tattoo and never tried to call her kids.

That all sounds so petty when I read it, but it is true. I hate that I have to be responsible for basic needs for her kids, while she hasn't been responsible for them in a very long time. Again, I don't understand someone putting anything above their kids, especially drugs. I think the biggest benefit that has come out of the situation is the fact that I now have pretty amazing relationships with each of her kids. My niece and I have never been as close as we are now. She feels that she can come to me with any problem, and knows that I will just listen. My oldest nephew now actually talks to me and loves on me when he sees me. And my youngest nephew has been more engaged with me over the last 7 months than any other time I can remember. I was being a disciplinary to these kids for so long, that they actually hated me. My niece has actually stated that she hated me, which just makes me laugh now. A few weeks ago, for the first time ever, my niece asked to come spend the night with me. It was an amazing thing, and I don't know if she understands how much it means to me to have her want to spend time with me.

Part of me resents my sister. She has changed the dynamic of my entire family, and I don't think she has any understanding of that. At this point, my parents are spending every day with my niece and nephews, my kids are lucky if we spend one evening a week with them. My parents are amazing, and they do not treat any of the children any differently, but I worry about my kids not getting it. My oldest has asked me several times why his cousins get to sleep at nana and pappy's (my parents) every night, but he never does. He's too young to understand what's going on, but is old enough to know that there are differences. I have to remind my mom at times that my kids deserve to have time with them as well. This isn't a slam at my parents at all, they are not supposed to be raising kids, I get that. But that doesn't change that I'm angry about it. I'm angry that my sister has stopped all responsibility for her children. I'm angry that when I take all the kids, including my own, to see her, she expects that everything is just going to be "normal". I hate that I've been left to manage our family needs, Mother's day, Christmas, birthdays, without any support from the one person who is supposed to be helping. My brother is in school in a different state, as well. So, if there are things that need to be done for the family, it is all on me. This is tough. There has been many nights that I have just cried, because it's hard to be the stable child in a whirlwind of chaos. My sister is the reason for this. Period. I understand that things should be different; I also understand that they never will be. I will forever be the responsible one, the one who has to manage the needs of our family, because I don't think she ever will be able to.

My sister has been sober since I dropped her off at detox in November. I have so many feelings about everything. I don't want to make her talk about anything from the past, but I know damn well that we will never have a relationship if we don't. And maybe that's okay. We will never be as close as we could have been, or once were, because there's just too much damage done. Maybe one day that'll change, but at this moment,

I have no real interest in having a relationship with her. She has been overly disrespectful to my mother, who is one of the only people who has honestly been there, through thick and thin. She has totally cut out my father, who has also been there for her. She tries to maintain a relationship with my brother, and maybe that's working. We don't talk about my sister much, because it just brings up too much shit, I guess. My sister has caused my husband and me to have endless disagreements. Thankfully he has gotten better at just listening to me vent out my frustrations, and not put in his two cents, unless he feels it'll be productive. I am proud of my sister for getting sober, but it is conflicted with anger that she ever started using drugs.

If you ask me my feelings on her today, I will tell you that I hate her. I hate what she has done to our family, what she has done to her kids, and what she has caused throughout the last few years. I guess hatred is better than ambivalence, and I guess that means at least I still care enough to hate her. I try not to think about her much because it breaks my heart. I have days that I can really see a difference in the person that she is. Those are the days that she asks me how I am and is actually interested. Or the days that I can call her and just catch up without crying at the end of the call. I also have bad days, which are more frequent right now. These are the days that my mom calls me crying because, once again, my sister has been mean to my mom, or the days that my dad tells me he has no feelings about her, whatsoever. I'm working through things on my own, with the support of my family. My parents have seen me cry and hate her more than anything. My brother, even from hundreds of miles away, has allowed me to cry to him and express my frustration. My husband has just been there every day, listening to everything I have to say.

I don't know what the future holds for mine and my sister's relationship. I'd like to tell you that eventually we will be close again, and that everything will be fine, but I don't know if that is true. All I know right now is that I need to focus on the positives that have come out of this. My relationships with my niece and nephews have improved tenfold, my mom has shown me how to be strong even when I want to crumble, my dad has been a support to me when I didn't think he would be able to talk about things, and my brother has grown up enough that I can talk to him as an adult, and have him understand what I need in the moment. My hope is that my sister can maintain her sobriety for the rest of her life. I hope that one day I can have a relationship with my sister that is better than what it has ever been. Maybe one day I will have my sister as my best friend.

I know that eventually my sister will want to make amends with me as part of her 12-step work. It'll be interesting to see how it goes. I've never been good at being honest with her, until recently. I guess that's another positive from the situation. Her addiction and our lack of relationship have made it much easier for me to be honest with her when things are hard to say. Our relationship is already shit, what difference does it make? I look forward to the day that I can look at her and tell her how proud I am of her for making it 10 years sober. I look forward to having my sister, sober, in my life. I look forward to seeing how she does being a mother sober, but I am going to be right there to step in if she can't do that for my niece and nephews.

I am the sister of a heroin addict, and that's okay.

September 27, 2017

Well I haven't looked at this since I wrote it in May 2017. My sister has now been sober for almost 10 months. I am currently not mad at her, and have actually enjoyed wonderful phone calls with her over the last week. We spent 2 hours on the phone one night, laughing until we cried, for the first time in years. I can see a difference in the person that she is. Her eyes are clear; she is much less agitated, and much more engaged with all the kids. Just the other night, she and my daughter looked at the stars together, in awe. I don't think my sister has enjoyed the stars in quite a while.

I thought about editing the first part of my chapter, but realized that it is so important for people to get that information. I hated my sister. I'm sure that I'll have times in the future that I hate her again, but hopefully it'll be normal sibling shit rather than shit related to drugs or her addiction. We've talked a bit about things that have happened in the past, but try not to dwell on them. We'll work through them over time, maybe. Maybe, we will just continue to try to make progress forward. I am more hopeful now than I was when I wrote the first part of the chapter. I think that I can see the person that I thought my sister would be. I remain cautiously optimistic that I will have a relationship with my sister.

I don't want to negate anything that I said previously. The biggest thing for me to understand is that it is okay for me to feel however I feel that day. I have some amazing people in my life that will listen when I am struggling, validate my feelings. Having a solid support system (family and friends) is so important through this process. My parents are dealing with a child with addiction issues, and they are not always able to support me in my more difficult times. I get it. I continue to try and be there for them as much as possible. Be strong for the people in your life, but also be strong for you. Things will get better. People do change, but it DOES take time.

I'm not sure what my relationship will look like with my sister in the future, but as it stands, it'll be okay. We will be able to talk, and laugh, and love each other and each other's children. I am hoping that she and my husband can mend their relationship at some point, simply because I want her in my life. It would be much easier if they were on good terms, as well.

I remain the sister of a heroin addict, and it continues to be okay. Things will never change the history we have, but we are working on making amends. Every single day.

Chapter 4

"I am the brother-in-law of a heroin addict."

When you are younger you think about one day being married. You have in your head a perfect, almost fairy tale type, life with a wife and kids, and acquiring a new family as your own. I have that and am blessed to have every one of them in my life. But how do you deal with one of those family members being a drug addict? I've asked myself that more than a few times.

I met my now wife when we were going into the sixth grade during summer rec. We became very good friends and stayed that way over the next ten years before we got together. We knew very quickly this was it and started doing the whole meet the families and all that good stuff. I met her mother, father and brother first. A short while later I met her older sister and her boyfriend. First impressions were not bad. I saw a fairly young couple with 3 kids and thought it was cool to have an older sibling, not having one myself. But fairly quickly my opinion of her sister and boyfriend started to change.

I noticed very quickly that the boyfriend was sketchy. He could never hold a job and was always "waiting on money to come in". Which, even still, some people aren't as fortunate as others with a job but I was raised to work and hold a steady job so, me being me, judged him for this and I don't feel bad about it. At the same time all of this was happening I also was being told my now sister in law was constantly borrowing money but was also going from job to job with some breaks in between. Again, I judged because I have been working over the table since I was 15 and mowing lawns since I was 12. It also blew my mind that a grown ass woman's parent would shell out so much money every single week. We all struggle, I get it, but this was crazy. She would make up some, to me, crazy bullshit story that didn't even make sense, AND THEY BOUGHT IT!!! I said on multiple occasions to my wife that what she was saying didn't even make sense or that it was a lie. It was shrugged off and forgot about. Until the next week, and the next, and the next. I saw that she was milking it, and I saw through her lies, but as an extended family member, who am I to say anything. And anytime I did, naturally, she was defended. So I threw my hands up and said, ok. I thought she was just blowing it on McDonald's and stuff for herself. This went on for about 4 or so years.

My sister in law's demeanor has, for the most part, either been like she's on screech and overly happy or kind of mellow. I don't think I've ever seen her in between. But I thought that's just how she was. I've never been exposed to someone on drugs, so my mind didn't automatically go there. But then she went from "borrowing" money, which she never intended on giving back, to taking it. She would be told no and she would take it instead, from her own family. Now I've gone to being judgmental of my sister-in-law to not respecting her, to being very angry at her. She stole from her parents, her grandmother, me and my wife, that I know of. She stole money from her parents, grandmother and my wife, and took a compound bow, to pawn, from me.

Naturally, someone gets something stolen, they press charges. But again, being an extended family member that put me in an awkward position. Do I press charges and piss off the rest of the family, including my wife? Or, do I keep my mouth shut and let her get away with it, like she had way too many times before? I didn't do a damn thing and just let it go. Enabling her to do more damage.

All this damage, we found out later, was caused because she had a drug habit to support. Without a job, she was relying on the ones that were supposed to be closest to her, against their knowing. I'm angry. I'm resentful. Most days, I hate her for what she's done to her family. My feelings aside, I'm blown away at how someone can do such awful things to their own family. She was high when she watched my oldest son. She was high at my wedding, where she was the maid of honor and made a terrible speech for my wife because she was too worried about her next fix to be bothered with writing a nice speech for her sister on her wedding day. She was high at the hospital when, not only my youngest son was born, but also my daughter. I'm angry and I have every right to be.

When she finally admitted she was a drug addict, she went to detox. I thought, well this isn't going to last. It didn't. She got "released" which is what she told everyone, which I think is a lie. She went right back into her same routine. A while later she finally went to a sober living home, where she is now. But that's not where my anger stops.

I can't remember if it was before she left for the sober house or after, but we started hearing stories from her kids. How on school nights, if they weren't left at home, she would bring them to "a friends" or just a random house where she had to go inside to do "work", very late at night. How someone can put their children in that type of situation is disgusting. Putting a drug habit before kids' safety is an all-time low in, my experience. But she's at a sober house now trying to get better. She's down there living it up. No kids, no worries, getting tattoos when she feels like it, going to the beach whenever she wants, going for random drives to wherever she feels like. All while her parents, who just had their last child leave the house, are now taking care of her three children. How can I not be angry or resentful?

My hands are tied. For the most part, I feel my role is to listen. My opinions are very blunt and I am very black and white on anything, so when it comes to this, I'm pissed. She's screwed over her family and it's a very long road to come back from that, if she is able to at all, in my opinion. She's on the road to recovery but I don't know if I have it in me to ever forgive her for what she's done. When everything started I thought "I didn't sign up for this". But the reality of it is, none of us did. Except her. She chose to take pills. She chose to do heroin. She chose to do cocaine. She chose, not us. So now I sit back, take it all in, and take it for what it is. I remember that I married my wife because I love her and try not to let any of this fucked up mess of a situation affect us. I hope she can get better if not for anyone else, at least for her kids, because I think they're too innocent and young to know what's gone on. Everyone has their own opinion and feelings about this. Whether it's your mother, daughter, sister or sister in law. My feeling on it is anger and resentment.

I am the brother-in-law of a heroin addict and I don't care much about her, but I want my wife to be happy again and so I am glad her sister is working so hard to get clean, that's it.

Chapter 5

"I am the brother of a heroin addict."

Being the brother of a drug addict is, by far, the most trying situation that I have ever been in. On one hand, my older sister was always looking out for me, checking on me, and making sure that I was happy. On the other hand, my sister has caused countless problems between my parents, had caused her children to be severely obese, and put her entire family in a dangerous situation.

When I was young, Nicole lived a five-minute walk from my home. Whenever I was bored after school or during the summer I could go see her and my niece. Nicole was always available to me and has taught me some incredible lessons, including being happy with what I have, rather than wishing for something intangible. That has been a key aspect of my persona growing into a young adult and made me a much more carefree and relaxed person. In my younger years, Nicole was one of the most influential people in my life.

When I got a bit older, I started hearing about some drug use when my parents would get mad at Nicole and they would argue, but it never seemed to be as tragic of a situation as it became. For a while the drugs were just an occasional argument in my mind. Then when she started getting arrested, and she always seemed to be in legal trouble, I knew that things were getting worse and starting to snowball. Eventually, Nicole went to detox, and according to her it worked. My family and I soon found out that was wrong, when she continued using heroin and gave her children to my parents. This was about the time I started to be angry with Nicole. How can someone give their children away? We have always had such a strong sense of family and family has always been such an important aspect of my life and she willingly gave it away.

I was home for summer break after my freshman year in college and I remember a time that totally scared me. Nicole's children were away for the weekend and my mom was recovering from a pretty big surgery. I got the call from my dad that Nicole was missing and my parents were at my grandmother's house. Nicole lived upstairs at this house, in an apartment, and my parents had been there for over an hour waiting to talk with her. My dad called because my mom was not feeling well and he needed me to come over. I get there and my mother is sitting in her bathrobe in a lawn chair trying to get comfortable and my dad is beside himself trying to care for her and worrying because no one knows where Nicole is. She has texted them and told them she is coming back in ten minutes but 40 minutes goes by with her as a no show. My other sister shows up and sends our parents' home so dad can take care of mom. She tells me, "I need you to come with me. We need to find her. Are you prepared for us to find her dead because that is why she is not showing up? She has taken so much, she doesn't want to see mom and dad and she may not make it this time and part of her doesn't want to make it. She is in a real bad way." We go everywhere we can think to find Nicole but we never did find her that night. I remember coming home that night and feeling helpless to fix this. I am very much like my dad and I fix things. This isn't anything someone else can fix, there is only one person and she didn't want it more than she wanted her next "fix".

I was away at college through most of the terrible times, but I have seen the damage she has caused. Being away, it was incredibly easy for me to cut her out of my life. I ignored her messages and phone calls, I thought of her as such an awful person, and had no thoughts of ever being sympathetic toward her. I have had to support my other sister through phone calls as she cries over losses and all she is having to shoulder for family responsibilities (which includes caring for 6 children sometimes so my parents can get away for a weekend, including weekends to come 12 hours south and watch me play lacrosse). This has made me feel guilty that I am not there to help her, but I know I need to do what my parents and siblings have always wanted for me. I feel torn at times. I feel sick at times. I feel sad at times. My parents deserve better. My sister and brother in law deserves better. My nieces and nephews deserve better.

Eventually, I started to think about it more and more. I stopped ignoring her and reformed our relationship. I have never been in a situation that could cause the harm that hers has, and I personally think that she has done amazing given the known difficulties of heroin addiction. My sister has gone from an amazing woman in my eyes, to the very bottom of the barrel, back to being my sister. Having watched this from afar I have been afforded the ability to be objective to the entire thing when I put thought into understanding this situation. After a while, I learned to control my emotions and found a way to become a support system for my sister so that I can someday see my niece and nephews loving their mother and their mother giving the children her entire effort, no distractions. When I finally see that, I will understand better why I wish to support my sister through her recovery.

I am the brother of a heroin addict and I am learning to live with her fall from who and what she meant to me in my life, to becoming one of the worst possible persons in my life, to rebuilding our relationship to love and respect each other and the strides she is taking to becoming just Nicole, my big sister.

Chapter 6

"I am the daughter of a heroin addict."

Saying that puts a hole in my heart. It is a label I don't deserve. I did not make this choice but I have paid a huge price for her actions. I have lost friends, I have had teachers look at me with pity, I have had to tell people on my cheer squad, I have had to explain why I am living with my grandparents, I have had to beg for money and support that should be coming from my parents, and I have been humiliated more than once by how my parents have acted.

In October of 2016, I am freshman in my high school, first semester, living with my grandparents already and it is Parent Night for my Cheer Squad. I am getting my first Varsity letter and my mother comes to the gathering looking like a strung out crack head. She is really skinny and her eyes have black circles under them and she doesn't smell good. I know she is high and I just smile and take the pictures and can't believe what she looks like in them. It is hard for me because she is acting like a teenager and demanding money from my grandmother (nana). I can't wait to be done and back to my grandparent's home. It is three more months from then before I can see a difference in her and start to enjoy being back with her.

It was fall of 2013, when we were in the car on my way to get dropped off at my friend's house for the night. My mom told me to look out the window, I knew what this meant, she was going to do drugs. Ever since I can remember my mom had done drugs but I didn't realize it was that big of a deal. I also didn't realize that that day was going to be the day I never looked at my mom the same.

"Do you know what I do for drugs?" She asked as I looked out the window.

"No,"

"Do you have an idea?" she sounded surprised at my answer to her previous question.

"No," I said again.

"I smoke and snort heroin," and just like that my whole world had changed. I knew from health class that heroin was one of the worst drugs out there, I also knew a lot of people used needles and I did not want my mom to do that. The rest of the car ride was pretty quiet after that. Once we arrived at my friend's house I got out of the car and gave her a kiss goodbye like it didn't faze me. But it did, like I said, my life changed with just 5 words rolled into one sentence.

I used to wish she didn't tell me, that way I didn't have to lie, because I really didn't know.

My mom always said, "I'd rather my kids know than have to lie to them," and at times, in certain circumstances, I agree with that. But, not in this case! What did she hope to accomplish? Was it done for me? No! It was done for her, like everything else in her life at that time. She is so selfish! How could she expect me to carry that burden, at 12? Was it a cry for help? Did she want me to report her to take the decision out of her hands? At freakin' 12?!!!!

After she told me what she does for drugs it all added up. Happy one minute, cranky the next. She would sleep until the afternoon at times, she would leave and come back early morning. She would have money for her, but not for us. Knowing the truth and noticing all this stuff made me hate her at times. Sometimes, she would have to run to a "friend" or her "boss'" to get something, and be in and out within 5 minutes. Other times she could be in there for up to an hour. Sometimes it would get so hot, sweat would be running down our faces or backs. She always took the keys and locked us in so I couldn't roll down the windows. We live up north, so sometimes it would get so cold, the boys and I would be shivering and trying to stay warm by sitting close together. If I called her to see what was taking so long, because either the boys were crying, fighting, or I just called her because I wanted to go home, she would get mad and would hang up leaving me to deal with my 3 and 4 year old brothers, who also wanted to go home, but were too young to figure out what to do.

I have two younger brothers, A., who is now 7 and W., 6. I watched them a lot of the time. I was often responsible for them for hours when I was only 12. They were really naughty kids. They would swear, hit me and each other. They would pee on the floor just for "fun", ride their bikes in the road or destroy things. I finally got a pair of glasses and one of the boys took them and broke them in half and just laughed. My mother said I should have taken better care of them, so two years went by without me having glasses. I would try and discipline them, and this would either get me in trouble by our mother because I "wasn't their mother" or I'd just get yelled at and called names by the boys. They basically ran the house and I was just there when my mom wasn't. They decided when they went to bed, and when they got up. They decided where they slept, and they never slept in their own room. They would make themselves so overtired they would pee the bed nightly, especially the older one, A. They chose dinner, lunch, and snacks. If they wanted to, they would have multiple meals. They were overweight and no one was doing anything to help them, or me. They were out of control, and so was my mother. One crazy life!!!!

In middle school is was hard to make "real friends," the kind of friends that you could tell all your secrets to, the ones that would help you through whatever you're going through. I had one real friend, she was my BEST friend. She didn't know about my mom or any of that but she would come and spend the night and I think she had a pretty good idea, but we never talked about it because she never asked. In middle school, I tried different after school sports and clubs. I played field hockey all through middle school. I also did drama. Usually, I was late being picked up or dropped off for practices or rehearsals. It was so embarrassing to always be the one that was late, or not picked up, and we never had money for the things those teams/plays needed me to get. My mom always made me beg for money from my grandparents, so I could help support her needs, as well as get the things I needed to be accepted by everyone. I hated it!

I lost my childhood best friend when she and her mom found out that my mom was doing drugs. We weren't allowed to hang out or anything outside of school, so we slowly drifted away completely. I tried to make different friends, but sometimes that got me in trouble, and of course it didn't matter that I'd get into trouble because my mom wouldn't do anything about it. My 7th grade year I got 3 suspensions, mostly for stupid things that were not even a big deal but, I never got into trouble at home so why stop being bad to impress my new "friends,"

My family was hard to be around. Before going to a family event or family get together my mom, most of the time, made me make up things that I needed money for so that when we left she could go and buy drugs. I'd lie to get her what she wanted/needed. I'd always look like I was asking for a lot though, but I wasn't, she was the one making me do the begging, I was not supported to be on a travel cheering squad because it cost too much money according to my grandmother but what she didn't know was that my mother and I were lying to get more money out of her to support my mom's addiction. I hated that because I really wanted to be a part of this squad, but it didn't happen for me.

I went through a phase were I hated my aunt, she was always so bossy, and really hard on me. She could see I was headed in the wrong direction. I also know now she knew what was going on with my mother. Now I realize she was doing it for my own good, because my mom wasn't looking out for me. Things got worse right before it all ended. But once it all ended it didn't really "end"

On October 1st, 2016 my friend, brothers and I were at a fair with the other family members when I got a text from another friend that lived down the road saying, "Hey is your mom okay?" I replied with "I don't know I'm not at home why?" I waited for a text back as my heart raced imagining the worst things possible. You cannot believe how embarrassed I was to hear this. "There are a BUNCH of cop cars at your house, just thought I'd check in" I called my mom and got no answer so I called my great grandmother who lived in the lower half of our house. When the phone was picked up it was my grandfather (Pappy). He didn't get into detail all he told me was that we wouldn't be living with my mom anymore but we would be living with them. Oh, no stress there!!!

When we returned home from the fair the next day we didn't see our mom, she was in jail. My brothers and I to this day (a little over a year later) still live with my grandparents. I still do not know what my mother did to get arrested, but it still embarrassed me because everyone at school knew she was arrested and that I was now living with my grandparents. I still worry she will go to prison and I won't be able to see her or understand when she will be free. Life sucked, really bad, right then.

Once it came out that we lived with my grandparents and people at school found out, I lost a lot of good friends. Parents were really angry that my mom was doing the drugs while their kids were with us. My mom stole money out of my best friend's wallet and she was only 14 years old. I was so embarrassed I asked my grandmother to replace it so she could get what she was saving for but it was so embarrassing. I found out that you can't trust even your "best" friend. That same friend told people at school humiliating details of both my life and one of my brother's intimate details. I have chosen to walk away from her, but it still hurts me because I never did anything wrong or to hurt her, but she feels she can say what she wants about me and my family.

When I moved in with my grandparents, it was hard to deal with the transition. A lot of things changed with rules, change of friends, and my grades were more of a stress than ever. My grandparents expected certain things that had never been expected of me and they also expected a regular schedule and discipline. I had never had these things, really. It was really hard, but so much nicer now. I know what is expected, they never change the rules, and they love me at all times, and have made me feel like I don't have to worry about anything except for my school and cheering. They take care of my brothers and never ask more of me then they do themselves. I have decided I am staying with them even when my mother gets better because I can then finish high school in the city where I grew up. I am thankful for that. They believe in me and my future. They expect me to do well in school and I do.

My grandfather asked me one night before bed how I was doing. I answered with the usual, "I'm good," when he said "Now, how are you really doing?" and that's when I looked at him and said "You know, it's really nice not having to worry about the boys late at night. My mom used to get them out of bed in the middle of the night and go get some drugs. I would hear them leave and get up and look out the window. I would lay awake until I heard them drive back in and I would see my brothers get out and stumble to go to bed upstairs. I hated that she would take them out at night. I feel so much relief that doesn't happen anymore and it's good to know we are all safe now." That was a huge step for me (us).

The scariest thing was that several of the guys my mom had around had started "flirting" with me. They were a lot older than me and were really weird. They would smile and try to touch me, but I just tried to stay away from them. My mom would let some of them live with her, off and on, and there were some scary and weird times with these men.

People have asked me why I never told my grandparents what was going on at my house with their daughter. I am not sure I can answer this. My Nana would love me to answer that question because she and my Pappy would have helped way earlier, but I don't really don't know???

I haven't missed a day of school or practice since I started high school in August of 2016. I push myself and work really hard on grades. I have amazing friends who are there for me without judgement. My brothers have lost about 26-29 pounds each. We have a dinner made for us every night, and our power is always on. My mom is now 10 months clean, her eyes are brighter, she's happy and she also has amazing friends that would do anything to help her come and see us. I am grateful for my mom's mistakes because it has taught me how to be strong and independent. We are all happier and healthier.

My family supports my brothers and me in any way they can, and my aunt that I once hated is now one of my best friends and biggest supporter. My mom now, is the best mom I've seen her be in my whole life. I will always love her and be happy she is my mom. I love that she had the strength and courage to get through it all. I don't deny that I can do these things because I'm strong and never had too many terrible things happen to me. I am bigger than the things that happened to me because of my mom's addiction. And I am grateful for all the love I have in my life.

You can fall into the same habits as your family or you can be a bigger, better person, it's all up to you and the way you look at life. I learned from my mom's mistakes and I refuse to fall into the same life that she had. I will not be a label, I will be who I am called to be, a survivor!!

I am the daughter of a heroin addict and I do not want my mom back, I want the new woman my mom is, as a recovered heroin addict, the one she is becoming everyday she is clean.

Chapter 7

"We are the sons of a heroin addict."

Disclaimer: This chapter is different as the boys are only 6 & 7 years old now. I (Nana) will be writing it for them in a statement/questions/answer type format so their perspective is heard. They are labeled A. for the oldest and W. for the youngest and the nickname for their sister is Sissy. They came to live with my husband and me when they were 5 & 6 years old, so their mother has not been present for any of their milestones like birthdays, Christmas or any other holidays for one year. She has seen the boys about once a month and attended when one had surgery on December 22, 2016, but other than that has not been able to participate in other events. She has come to sporting events, occasionally, and is trying to get to see those regularly now. Here's their story;

October 2nd, 2016

W: (5):   Jumping into the car, "Why are we going with you Nana? Where is mom?"

Me: "Hey honey, we are just going to be together for some time now. You mom is not well and needs to get better." I try to smile back at them but I am holding back tears as I know how hard this is going to be. "Sister will be with us at the house so you all three will be together and help Pappy and I do it right."

A: (6):   "Did mom get arrested again?" He asks with knowledge way beyond his years. "I knew she was sick again because she falls asleep all the time and won't talk or look at me and when she talks it doesn't sound right."

W: Still not understanding, "Where am I going to sleep? Am I going to see her before I go to bed?"

Me: "I have set up the spare room for you and A." Desperately trying to reassure him, he is younger and not so experienced and nonchalant as his older brother, "You have a bed and soon we will bring the bunk beds down so you can have your beds back."

W: "When? I haven't seen mom in days." (They had just gotten back from a 3 day weekend with the other grandparents. Nicole, their mom, got arrested on the Saturday night of that weekend.)

Me: "I know, we will see her in couple of weeks and we can try for next weekend to bring your beds down to my house." I am trying to refocus him until we can get back to home where my husband is so we can navigate this together, "How did it go at the fair?"

A: "Oh good, we had fun and did a lot of things with Meme and Papa." He said this all with a huge smile.

W: With his voice wobbling a little, "Are you sure we are not seeing mom? I would like to see her soon."

Me: "I know honey but we are just going to be together and let your mom get better." I pull over and go to the back seat and give him a big hug, "We are going to be fine. You are going to be fine."

W: Silent

A: "Hey are we going to get on the bus at your house now? That will super cool."

W. had more difficulty transitioning, but it amazed us how quickly he adjusted, and he showed super resilience to this situation. A. clearly showed more disconnect to the problems and situation he found himself in at this time. He almost treated it as a grand adventure, but this was just a shield. It falls apart later, but it appeared that he had so many transitions that this was just another and no big deal. I tried to have the boys see Nicole at least once every week to ten days, but she worried it was hard on them. Any time we left her, the boys picked right back up where we left off before they saw her.

This is a warning to all parents, when a child feels loved and cared for, when he knows that adults are in charge and going to keep them safe, when he doesn't need to worry, their allegiance can change quickly. It doesn't mean it can't change back but, it may not ever come back. And this is right and a form of justice, because you were given a precious gift, but your addiction was more important. You forgot the basic rule of parenting, when you have a child, your needs, desires, wants, etc. are put on the back burner for a period of time. Not always, and not forever, but for a time, and that is how it should be to parent and we should be joyous for the opportunity to be selfless.

Their story continued;

November, 2016

A: "Nana", A. called out from the back seat, "Do you remember the time I got hit by the car when I was riding it in the road?"

Me: "I do. I was so scared." The memory clearly coming back to me when he was rushed to the hospital a few months earlier. "I was sad for you and the woman who hit you. When you got hit by the car, were you wearing a helmet?"

A: With a touch of sassiness, "No, mom said I didn't need to wear it if I was in the yard. I told her I don't like to wear it." After a few seconds he said while looking at me from the corner of his eyes, "And why were you sad for the lady who hit me? She was in the wrong, she hit me."

Me: Knowing this was an important, teachable moment, I hesitate to answer him, then state firmly, "No A., you were in the wrong for going out in the street without permission, for showing no caution going out in the road on your bike, for not having control over your bike and for not wearing your helmet. It must have been scary for her to not be able to stop in time so she wouldn't hit you."

A: Silence

Me: After a minute or two of silence, I asked, "Where was your mom?"

A: "She was upstairs sleeping or something." He is looking out the window as if nothing is wrong or nothing has sunk in about this situation. "Sissy had to find her. She took me to the hospital to get checked out though when she came down."

Me: "Hmmmmmm!"

A: "Don't worry Nana, I was fine." He says this all as if getting hit by a car is no big deal and the fact his mom can't be found is just another day in his life. "Just some bumps and bruises. The doctor said it could have been a lot worse."

Me: While waiting for a light to change, I look back at him and smile right into his beautiful brown eyes and say, "I am glad it wasn't, sweetheart. We all love you so much."

A: "I think my mom loves me a lot, do you?" looking back into my eyes.

Me: "I do, honey."

A: My dad does, too. I know they love me."

Me: "Me too." (Very hard for me to say-Mom in detox, dad in prison.)

A: "Yeah, when my dad gets out from prison, he is going to buy me a four wheeler, and teach me how to be a roofer, we will go up in the big woods and cut down trees." (He continues on a litany of the things his father has told them they will do once he gets "out". The father is in for two more years at the time of this conversation, which means he will have been incarcerated for almost four years by the time A. will be 8 years old.)

W's Surgery;

December, 2016-Nicole 4 weeks clean and sober

Me: As we are driving an hour away to W.'s specialist appointment, "Are you excited to see mom, kids?"

All 3:   "Yes", "Yeah", "Can't wait"

Me: "Just everybody remember," trying to set the tone for the appointment, "This is an appointment to get W's surgery done, so make sure you all let your mom listen in the appointment. Sissy, you and A. will wait in the waiting room, then we will all go have lunch together so you can visit with your mom."

W: Curiously, "Do you know, Nana, if I am having this surgery?"

Me: "Yes honey, it should have been done about two years ago, lovey."

W: "OK." He accepts this without question but his worry comes out next. "Will mom be there when it happens?"

Me: "Yes, it has to happen here in the 'big city' because of the type of surgery it is and this is where your mom is staying, so she will be right there with you." Trying to be reassuring, "I will be there, and Uncle too."

W: "OK. I am glad and I am really glad Uncle will be there."

After the Appointment Where it is Confirmed Surgery is happening;

W: He stopped in the hallway outside of exam room, "Mom, I am going to have the surgery, right?"

Nicole: "Yes." She said smiling down at him, holding him close around his shoulders.

W: "You promise to be there." He doesn't move forward, waiting for her to answer.

Nicole: "Yes, I wouldn't miss it." Kneeling down next to him, "I want to love you while you go through this. We all want it done and over with now." (Very private surgery, very uncomfortable for him.)

W: "Mom you promise not to be late, or to not show up, or keep going outside, or talking on the phone. I am going to need you!" He says this last statement as he reaches up to her shoulders and almost shakes her.

Nicole: *Silence*

Me: Seeing her distress, I calmly say, "W., would it make you feel better if we pick her up? That way we all can get there on time and together."

W: "Yes, Nana it would, ok mom?"

Nicole: "Yes, that would be perfect. No worries then and we can all be together." (She cried on my shoulder in private before the kids and I left her and headed back to my house. This conversation with him really hit her hard. She kept saying she couldn't believe she had been such a terrible mom because she now is clear enough mentally to know that is exactly what it was like for the kids-her not being there.)

His surgery went perfect and Nicole was everything a mother should have been to W. He felt very loved and cared for through a very hard time for him. My husband was furious when she put it out on social media with pictures. He stated something to the effect of, doesn't she have any understanding of his need for privacy and she said many people were praying for him and she wanted to let them know he was out and fine even though he was very sore. This proved to be the last straw for the 2 of them, she blocked him, and he has blocked her from his life. Sad, and more devastation.

A's Surgery

January, 2017 (All 3 children hadn't had teeth cleaning in a couple years-First teeth cleaning for A.)

A: "Nana, I am glad we are going to the dentist, my teeth hurt." he said holding his cheek.

Me: With my face set and rigid because it sad to think of him in pain because Nicole so selfish. "Good, we will find out what is wrong."

A: "I think it is going to be a good appointment because we now brush our teeth twice a day, floss and use fluoride." Hoping he just remembers the good and not me yelling and all the crying and anger he showed when trying to get him to really brush his teeth.

Me: "Yup, you and W. do. I am so proud of you. You have really accomplished this skill of brushing your teeth. Remember how you would just pretend like you were brushing when you first came to live with me?"

A: "Yes, I do remember but my teeth hurt when I brushed, "holding his cheek again. "Now I know I need to take care of them. I also like the way I smell."

Me: "What?" I say laughingly. "What do you mean the way you smell?"

A: "I smell good," as he holds up his sleeve and smells it. "My clothes smell good and I am looking good too. Can you help momma to make sure we shower every night with our shower gel. And no smoking anything in the house (?). And also wash my clothes every week like you do?" He is smiling the whole time he rattles off the list of things I need to make sure happen when he returns to his mom.

Me: "You bet, buddy. She has already asked me to help her with that because she can see how good you are doing and she wants to do the same."

A: "Good and I want my hair cut like this. I look better with this haircut then just buzzed off with mom's clippers."

Me: With a sense he needs to understand where they were in the past, "I think mom did that because she didn't have money to take you to the hair place, but I can still help you get the cut you want, once you go back to mom, no stress."

A: Rolling his eyes, "Yeah, she was spending her money on other things."

After the X-rays and exam

Dr. M.:   Entering the exam room our dentist doesn't' make eye contact and asks A., "A. can I talk with your nana for a few minutes?" He just nods as he is having his first teeth cleaning.

Me: "Sure, I will be right back buddy. Just hang out and finish with your cleaning."

Dr. M.:   After she and I walk around the corner. "We have a big problem. He has nine teeth with cavities."

Me: Incredulously, "You mean he has nine cavities?"

Dr. M.:   "No he has nine teeth with cavities; several have more than one in it. He has to go to a pediatric dentist who will put him under to fix them all at once, if they can. It is the only way to do it humanely. And some are in permanent teeth, I am not sure the teeth can be saved." After, I thought she said it so fast just to get it out knowing how I would take it.

Me: "What? This is devastating!" (I start to cry and she hugs me and says it will be all right. Not one of my children ever had one cavity in their childhood because we took them to the dentist every 6 months, they had sealants and braces and Hyrexes, etc. all to ensure that they never had bad teeth. I cry 4 more times that day thinking about the pain he must be in, all the time, and the disappointment in my daughter. There is no denying this circumstance as something other than not being a responsible parent to this child, as anything but neglect. It is a breaking point for me.)

March 1st, 2017

A: All excited for this new adventure to get his teeth fixed, "Pappy, do you think it is going to hurt to get my teeth all fixed?"

Pappy: "That is what we are trying to prevent by having you go to sleep. That's why you couldn't eat, but remember, we will have lunch after when you feel better."

A: "Good, I am glad you will be with me. Nana, are you ok not going in with me?"

Me: "Yes, all our kids preferred Pappy over me during procedures like this so I am sure it will be the same for you." He really loves one on one with my husband so this is a big deal for him, he has had very little time in his life with a responsible male figure. "I will be in the waiting room and see you right after it is done."

The procedure goes well but he is not under so much that he doesn't writhe in pain at the two largest cavities and they do pull one of his permanent teeth in the back because it is just breaking apart while they work on it. All the rest where corrected. It was one of the hardest things for my husband to witness through this year. He has said it will be one thing he will never forgive Nicole for, her neglect of this child's teeth. I won't either, even writing and re-reading makes tears well up in me as I think of the constant pain he must have been in through the years. That night, A. had some amazing things to say about his teeth.

Pappy: As we all sit down to eat supper, "How's your teeth doing buddy? Are you ok?"

A: "Pappy", with amazement in his voice, "this is the first time I remember eating and not having pain in my teeth. It is wonderful."

Pappy: "So are you glad you did it? Do you remember anything from the procedure?"

A: "No not a thing, I am so glad we did it. My teeth are great." He continues to tell us how wonderful it is to have his teeth done. His next appointment he had one small cavity that they think was under the gum line, otherwise his dental hygiene was perfect.

W's Memories of Trips to Their Uncle 12 hours south

May, 2017

W: "Hey Nana, do you remember last year going to watch Uncle play lacrosse at college?"

Me: "Yes I do. We also went to Hershey for the first time." This was the first real trip they remember.

W: "That was fun seeing Uncle. You were mad at mom, do you remember that, too?" Looking out the window he was very happy looking, "She was having issues!!"

Me: "That sounded funny. Where did you hear that word, issues?"

W: "That is what she would call it when she wasn't doing good. She would just tell me not to worry, she was just having issues." He rolled his eyes and stuck his tongue out towards the window.

Me: "Well, those "issues" you are talking about were what made me mad at your mom so I do remember that."

W: "Maybe next year, she can come with us to watch Uncle play in a game. I have gone two times and she has never even gone once." He leans his head back to look at the sky. "I would love for her to come with us."

Me: "Yes, that would be super. I don't know if she can come, it is a whole year away."

W: Wistfully sighing, "Well, I hope so. I can show her all sorts of things." After a few minutes of quiet he asks me, "Do you think we will be back with her by then?"

Me: Sighing too, "I hope so, honey. She is doing really well and she can't wait for you all to be back together."

W: Looking out the window, "Yeah, me too, me too, Nana."

The boys finished their school year with many improvements in their scholastic work, behaviors and social skills. The teachers and principle can't believe the change in the boys' appearance and attitude. We have gotten nothing but support and kindness from them, to us, and even Nicole. They have worked hard to keep her in the information loop, which she and I have appreciated. In our next book, regarding the extended circle around the addict, the teachers and K's cheering coach, have all consented to write a chapter together about what it has been like to watch the children of people struggling with addiction through this journey of recovery.

W and A's Biggest Worry

Before the boys moved in with us, my husband and I would fondly call them the butt brothers because the crack of their asses would be hanging out all the time. They were not the only ones in our household that would happen with, their mom and dad, occasionally my son, and others would have the same problem. "Say no to crack!", and "Crack is whack!" had totally different meanings at our house. It wasn't until after they moved in that I find out why they had so much trouble keeping it undercover. They had always been big, heavy boys. Both of their parents are larger people, so I didn't question it too much, but it was very apparent that they were obese. When I started feeding them, they would not eat a lot of food and really preferred processed food. I remember A. would get pukey with certain foods and textures, like rice or pork chops. He wouldn't try real food or whole grain breads. W. would eat until he felt sick. He loved sugary juices and soda.

Things changed for them. They have converted to a healthier diet, more exercise and learned portion control. Over this last year, A. has lost 29 pounds and W. 26 pounds, and both have maintained the weight loss. They have clothes that fit them and have learned where pants are supposed to sit on your body. They are proud of their bodies and feel fit and strong. They can run for long periods of time, and play all day long outside. Their doctors, teachers, and other family members can't believe it. No where do they go without people saying how wonderful they look today. A., the older, has become the king of getting the flags in flag football and W., the younger, is a super lacrosse player like his Uncle, my son. Their overall health has so improved that they look like totally different children. Their biggest fear is returning to their mother and regaining all their weight. This is also Nicole's (their mother) biggest fear. I am sending menus and calendars full of ideas for real food for the boys to eat when they return to their mother, but all of us worry that they will return to obesity.

June, 2017;

W: "Nana, can you talk to my mom?"

Me: "Sure, honey. About what?" Hardly listening as we are super busy getting supper together.

W: "I don't want ever to be fat again." I stop and listen to him, looking him right in the eye. "I like my body and I can run so fast now."

Me: Slowly and carefully I respond, "Yes, you can. You are like superman zooming all over the place."

W: "I don't want to ever look like I did. Some of the other kids made fun of me and called me fat. I am strong now, not fat. No one calls me fat now. Remember when I told you I didn't like pullover sweatshirts? That was because I took one off last year, and when my t-shirt went up, a girl saw my stomach and laughed and told the other kids how fat I was under my clothes." He dropped his head and then looked back up to me.

Me: I let him see my tears that immediately come to my eyes, "Oh, W., I am so sorry that happened. I will talk to your mom, but you need to hear that she has already talked to me about not wanting you guys to ever gain back that weight. She is very happy that you are so healthy and she wants to keep that up." I want him to know we are all worried about it and are on it. "Want to help me make a calendar with meals and activities so you can all follow it?"

W: "Yup, that sounds great. Did you see that dump truck that just went by? It was huge." So quick to move on because he is reassured we are all on it.

W. has continued to bring this topic up but never with the clarity of the day. A., has the same worry although his is more complex. It is my husband's theory that A. seeks out food as a comfort and if he could, he would eat until he gets sick. A. is very focused on food, to the degree he watches food all the time. I know that sounds weird but he literally watches food like he is getting some secondary gain in his brain. Even after he has just eaten something, he asks about the next food he is going to eat. If he were not supervised, he would eat non-stop, we believe. He went to eat with his great-grandmother at a fast food restaurant, and she let him order two main course menu options, fries and a shake for a total of 1752 calories for one meal. After this event, I spoke with the entire family about ensuring good food choices if the boys are with them, and I guess I was "forceful enough" that they all report to me everything they fed them. Even the other grandparents and their family members see the difference and work very hard to feed them appropriately, which doesn't mean no ice cream but limited amounts of any sweets and using whole, real food. It feels like everyone is on the same team and that team is health for the boys. If allowed though, A. would always eat like that and could easily gain the weight back in 3 months

In an attempt to help shift this focus, I have started to teach him how to cook with fresh items, whole food from scratch. A. has a lot of interest in the preparation of his food, which is a big change. With his teeth being fixed, he can now eat vegetables and fruit that are hard, and non-processed food. He loves them, but all of us worry that Nicole will not continue this line of thinking and behaving. We now know that they can be healthy and should not be so heavy, so it should be easy enough to monitor but, it is a stress to all of our family.

A: Getting ready before school, "Nana, do you think I look good in these khaki shorts?"

Me: "Yes, I do. You look great. Let's look in the mirror to double check."

A: Turning side to side in the mirror. "I do look good in these. Did you know they are two sizes smaller then I used to wear?" (He now has huge pride in how good he looks.)

Me: "Yup, you look great." Deciding to give him something else to be proud of, "I have something funny to tell you. You now wear the size W. was when you came to live with me and now he doesn't have much to wear. He needs to get some new clothes, but you are getting hand-me-ups." He starts to beam and laughs out loud.

A: "Nana, I have never heard of that. Is that what it really is called?" He can't really believe it and continues to grill me about it. "I am the size W. used to be and he is so small he needs new clothes. That is hilarious!"

Me: "I guess I better at least get you one new shirt and shorts outfit, huh? In your new, smaller size."

A: "I am never going to be fat again." As we walk downstairs to get breakfast, "Did you know my dad is smaller too? He says in prison that he only gets so much food and he works out all the time so he has gotten skinnier."

Me: (Stunned at the switch in conversation) "No, honey I didn't know that. I am hoping you are learning what food to eat to stay healthy and to keep you running and playing your sports so well."

I spend a lot of time skimming these kinds of land mines. I try not to disrespect their mom and dad, but there are times it is important to remind them that their life is not the way it should be right now because of their parents' choices. My husband has started a really good way of reminding them by focusing it more on the boys' choices. He consistently says that it is all about choices, reminds them where their parents are living and then restates it is all about choices and the boys are going to have to make their own in the future. I use this same strategy now for everything from food choices, to how you sit on the bus, to how you treat others, and they have started using it back to me, telling their choices of the day.

We are the sons of a heroin addict and we just want our mom back.

I guess in closing up their chapter, it is clear to me that of all the people affected by the heroin addict, the children pay the hugest price. I have always known this in my intellect, but watching the boys struggle to continue to love parents that really don't deserve their love or the worries they have been burdened with through the years, the near death experiences, the potential and real abuses they have endured, it comes home to seep into my mind until the fear for their future overwhelms me at times. I do not want to continue to raise them, nor does their mother want that for her boys. This was never a hostile take-over. But, the real threat of that happening is ever present, until she proves she can do it and not relapse or abuse them again. The family lawyer involved in this case has told both Nicole and I that my husband and I have enough documentation from this year, and the children's' health has so improved, that we could petition the courts for custody, and would be given it. That is not what is wanted or being looked at, but I will never let this happen again to the boys. She has one shot at being the mother she has been called to be and how she was raised to be. Only one!! And I believe with all my heart, she will be the good mother she can be. I have to believe it or I couldn't make it through another day. I need her to do it, so pray she does do it.

Chapter 8

"And I am the heroin addict"

Holy shit. I really don't know where to begin. I guess I'll start by saying I am a heroin addict who is trying to get clean. I've been on either dope (heroin) or pills since I was about 19 or 20 and I'm now 32. I would like to make it clear that this is in no way, shape, or form my parents' fault. I never had a big trauma that I felt the need to hide under getting high. I really had (and very luckily still have) an amazing family who is crazy supportive and good to me. Not that I deserve it, but I'm very grateful for it.

I suppose I should give a bit of history. I've had chronic back pain as long as I can remember. It's a pain that's always been there, but normally was tolerable. When I would have a flare up, I'd go to my doctor who would give me a small prescription of Hydrocodone. Normally, I would take it before bed for a few days, and then get rid of the rest. I had moved out of my parents' house at 19, in August of 2003, to move in with my then boyfriend, who was 23. I later found out that this guy had not only JUST gotten out of prison, but has always been a regular marijuana smoker and would mess with any and every drug he could get. Anyway, shortly after moving in with him, I had a flare up. I went to the doctor and got Hydrocodone.

When I got home, my boyfriend, who we will call E, asked me for a few. I was confused, as I did not at all like them. He told me that if I took some then "fought the fatigue" when it passes that I would feel really good. So, of course, being young and completely stupid, that's just what I did. One 5 mg Hydrocodone make me feel so in love. I literally had no problems. I cleaned my entire house, organized shit I had put off for months, I loved it. For the first time in my entire life I was calm, energized, and just absolutely...peaceful. If only I knew this is where it would lead me!

So, for many, many months I'd call for refills and get them. We connected with other people who took pills. I clearly remember driving to get some off a friend when I had run out early, like always. I called her when I was close to her house and said, while laughing, "We've done these Vics so many days in a row that I actually feel high NOT being on them!" We both laughed, I continued on my way to get them from her. If only I knew I'd end up a lost, broken heroin addict. If only I could go back to that day. I try really hard to tell myself that everything happens for a reason, but fuck, what good reason could there possibly be to waste 14 years of a great life being dependent on drugs?? I'm hoping for some clarity to come to me over the next couple months. Good God, I need clarity.

I'm going to fast forward to 2016 for a minute here. I am now on heroin, every single day. In the spring, I had gotten caught a few times taking money and checks from my family. I had taken a check from my nana, so my dad was at her house, as was I, discussing it. Dad asked me why I had done it, for the millionth time, but instead of coming up with a story, I looked at him, dead in the eyes, and said "Dad, I'm a heroin addict!" This was the first time I'd ever told anyone in my family. He later told me that he and my mother had figured

I was on drugs, but obviously couldn't prove it (and I wasn't admitting it) and it was actually a relief to know I wasn't just dumb and insane since I kept stealing and doing stupid shit. Anyway, Dad called my mom, who was already close to my nana's house. I could hear my mom on the phone, she also sounded relieved. My Aunt was also close and came into this conversation. She has also been a HUGE part of my journey. Once everyone was there, they asked what my plan was. I told them that first I had to go to detox, as I knew I was going to be really, really sick, though I'd never gone more than 16 hours without using until this point.

Luckily (again), the very next day my kids (I have three. I'll explain in a few) were leaving with my mom to go on a road trip 12 hours south to see my little brother. He was going to a great college and the kids and mom were going to watch him play a lacrosse game, going to Hersey Park, and doing all kinds of fun things. So, I made the decision to go to a detox unit at a hospital in a city about 35 minutes from our home, the very next day. My aunt immediately offered to bring me, which I accepted. That night I explained to my kids what was happening, in age appropriate terms, as much as I possibly could, and I packed a bag.

Jumping back again, I feel I need to explain my family dynamic. Also, please understand as I am writing this, I am planning my final detox and rehab to begin the next stage of my life. That said, I am writing this as things go through my head, and just tonight I have used both Cocaine and Heroin. My mind, body, and soul are a fucking mess. I hate these drugs (and myself) just enough more than I love them. Back to my point…I am currently a single mother of three. My daughter, my oldest is nearly 15. I had her my senior year of high school, 1 month and 5 days after I turned 17. I was not at all who you would expect to be a teen mom. I came from a well-respected, well off family. I was an athlete, decent student, I didn't party. My boyfriend was a little more wild than me, but he also came from a well-respected family. They had plenty of money, and owned a successful business.

I found out I was pregnant in the spring of my junior year. My boyfriend and I decided to have an abortion. I found out it cost $350 for it and it was done every week on Thursdays. It took a little bit for us to come up with that much money, but we did it. We went in to have my appointment, and they said they couldn't do it because I hadn't had all the labs done, which I wasn't told about. I began to cry because I knew I was close to the 12 week cut off since it took a while to come up with the money. They told us they would do it if I was a few days over 12 weeks since I didn't know and they absolutely had to have the labs to get my blood type in case something went wrong. So, we left the clinic and went directly to the hospital. I had my labs drawn and waited for the time next week. The following Thursday we returned to the clinic, where we were told that since I was 12 weeks and 2 days along they could not do it. What the actual fuck? We argued with them, explaining what we were told the week before, but they just did not give a fuck. At all. So, since we wanted to go to prom, we decided not to tell our parents until after prom. We went back to our regular stuff; school, hanging out, etc. Not long before prom I was on the phone with my boyfriend and suddenly felt crampy in my lower stomach, then felt wet, like I had started my period. I told him to hang on, went to the bathroom, and found I was in fact bleeding, bad, with lots of clots and kind of skin colored pieces. I was devastated and ecstatic. And relieved. I went back and told him I was currently having a miscarriage and apparently we were all set.

Now, since I was young and stupid, and hadn't told my parents, and didn't want to be in trouble, I never went to the doctor or told anyone, except my boyfriend. Summer came and went. I began my "period" again, though it was irregular and short. I went back to school in late summer, and my boyfriend and I broke up. We had been going to different schools, but senior year we both went to vocational school. He told me it wasn't going to work because we were seeing each other too much. I had my birthday on October 8th, then that weekend my mom and I went to clean my Nana's house. Mom called me into the bathroom and asked if I was pregnant. I explained to her that I hadn't had sex in many months, so I didn't think I was because if I was I would have been WAY pregnant. She said she was taking me to the doctors Monday because if I wasn't, there was something wrong with my stomach. I really didn't think I was pregnant, so I didn't stress too much. I had noticed that I wasn't able to lose weight in my stomach since the "miscarriage" but assumed it had just changed my body or something.

That Monday, we went to the doctors. Mom explained her concerns, and I peed in a cup. The doctor I was seeing went to get the results, and announced as she came back through the door that I was, in fact, pregnant. I nearly hit the fucking floor. She proceeded to try, unsuccessfully, to find the babies heartbeat. Awesome! So, not only am I pregnant, apparently, I am pregnant with a dead baby. They scheduled me for an ultrasound a couple of days out. There I found out that this baby was, in fact, very active but breech (head up/feet down) and I was due mid-December. Later, I talked to my doctor about the "miscarriage" and she explained that I had been pregnant with twins and only lost one. Apparently this is really pretty rare to lose one twin but not the other, especially at 14 or 15 weeks, but what I described was exactly that.

Fortunately, I was already enrolled at the vocational school, which had a daycare, and is where most teen moms go with their babies. The next few weeks, I have no memory of whatsoever, but I believe it was business as usual. November 12, 2001 was a day off from school, and my dad's sisters came over to help me clean my bedroom, set up the changing table and crib, and got my room ready for baby's arrival, even though I wasn't due for over a month. Thankfully they did, because at 4:00 in the morning, I woke up in extreme pain, all wrapped up in my sheets and blankets. Normally, I sleep still, so I had obviously been in pain and rolling around for a while. I waited a few minutes, the pain stopped, and I tried to go back to sleep. Then it hit again. I waited for it to stop again, and ran upstairs to get my mom. I felt like I was dying and the baby was dying. My mom is a nurse, and unless you were dead, dying, or bleeding out, she didn't worry too much (I say this with great love and affection). So I told her I was dying. She told me dad would be up in an hour, gone to work in an hour and a half and to go back to bed and relax and she would come and check on my when he left.

I did as I was told, but began timing these pains, and cursing Dad to move his ass out the damn door! By the time he did and mom came in, the contractions were 11 minutes apart. She said "Well sounds like this baby is coming out, and if she does you sure as hell don't want to be looking like that, so go take a shower and I'll start calling the family". A shower?? I'm dying and she wants me to take a SHOWER?! But I did as I was told, stripped and sat on the toilet waiting for a contraction, jumped in the shower, and was back on the toilet waiting for the next one. By the time my mom and I made it to the hospital, my entire family was there, along with my ex-boyfriend and his mother.

September 20, 2017. That is as far as I got in writing my story when I was getting high. I feel like that was really typical, I would start things out strong, then just leave them unfinished. I ended up having my daughter by c-section, and she was a healthy 8lbs 9oz on November 13. She was, and still is, an amazing human, whose spirit never ceases to amaze me. I will go back and explain the next 15 years or so, between the birth of my daughter and November 29, 2016.

I was given the Hydrocodone previously mentioned. Continued on that for a few years. During those years, I held a steady job, maintained the relationships in my life, including with E. We had a pretty successful construction company, and I worked full time. I went to college for medical assisting, and graduated with decent grades. Somewhere in the mix, we both got severely addicted. I remember when it came to the point when we had to first buy 30 mg oxycodone because there was nothing smaller available. I said to E that I wasn't able to break it down small enough, but went with the plan because I didn't feel well not having anything. Soon, we were buying 30 regularly. And by regularly, I mean every day. During this time, I got pregnant with A. He was somewhat planned, even though we were both still using apparently we felt it was a good time to go ahead and have a baby. I was able to secure a prescription for Hydrocodone again during my pregnancy, so I wasn't sick and they didn't bother to drug test me because they already knew I was taking the meds. When A. was born, he did have some signs of withdrawal, but it was nothing like the babies born addicted to suboxone or other drugs. He was a little fussy, and wanted to suck on a pacifier all the time, which is apparently signs of withdrawal in newborns. He weighed in at 8lbs even, and was otherwise healthy and today is a strong almost-8 year old boy, with a very funny, dry sense of humor, tons of love to give, and while he's a bit defiant sometimes, he is great.

Shortly after he was born, I started crushing up the 30s and snorting them. This gave a much more intense high, and I liked the feeling. E had been doing this for some time, and though I was angry about it at first, I fell right in line with it. I still was able to maintain a job, relationships and my life in general.

When A. was three months old, I got pregnant with W. Again, I used my entire pregnancy. He was born fine, but he was tongue tied and with a kind of "weird look" to him. (He is so very handsome, smart and funny, his "weird look" was possibly just due to the fact he was born with a mullet and it looked strange until I cut it.) This is around the time that things started to change for me. Until this point, my life was very manageable. I was a functioning addict, whatever that means. By society's standards, I was doing well. Had money, a house, family that was around, and had made my own little family.

This is also around the time that I began to struggle to find pills. When W. was between a year and two years old, E told me he wasn't able to find any pills, but he could get heroin. He explained that it was the same feeling as pills, but much cheaper. I tried calling everyone I knew to get pills from, with no avail. I again agreed to get the heroin. I did my first line of heroin and I was absolutely in love. I loved everything about it. The taste, the high, the price. It was exactly what I was hoping to find.

From that point on, heroin was everything. I was so very selfish. I would beg, borrow and steal from everyone and anyone to get it. I needed it to survive. I needed heroin like you need air. Like you need food. I stopped eating and lost a huge amount of weight in a short amount of time. I was totally ok with this as I had been bigger my whole life, and this new "heroin chic" look was wonderful. E was steadily using needles, I was still snorting mine. We would fight so badly about drugs. Who has more, who worked harder to score, and we turned on each other, because our true love was now the drugs.

Towards the end of the oxy use, we began selling one of his family member's pills. We told her they were way cheaper than they really were and mostly just kept them for our own use. This continued on for years, even as recently as summer 2016. This was the beginning of my selling.

E was a very good criminal. He would steal anything that wasn't nailed down, and some things that were. He did this for an extended period until he was caught and went back to prison. In the interim there were huge fights. We were both very abusive, and while I will not go into that here, there was a lot to deal with. But none of that mattered because we would just get high again and forget about it and think we were in love again. Please understand, it is very difficult for me because we spent 10 years of our lives together, had some amazingly good times, then in the last three years it all just fell apart. People ask why abused people don't just leave. The answer is painfully simple. There is always hope it will go back to how it was, that it will get better. Nobody gets into a committed relationship when things are bad. People are loving and caring, and when things do go bad, you remember the good times and hope things will return to that. This is too much to get into right here, so we will move on.

As I said, heroin was my love. I put it before anything and anyone, and refused to; thought I was incapable to; live life without it. The utter hopelessness in addiction is unbearable. Sitting on my bed writing this out, it makes my heart physically hurt to remember the feelings (or lack of feelings) involved and know there are addicts and families out there still suffering. I was not able to see any hope in any situation and had no faith there was a way out. I thought I was going to die a junkie. I wanted to die, simple as that. At one point I was given the opportunity to get a tattoo for free, and found one that's an Ambigram (says one word looking one way, and another word looking for the opposite way) that had the words faith and hope written in it. I knew I needed this tattoo and had it put on my left inner wrist. This was literally all the faith and hope I had. I remember laying on a "bed" in jail, with tears streaming down my face, having the realization that those were nothing but words to me with no weight behind them. Today, many tattoos later, this is still my favorite.

I'm not really sure when it happened, but when E started shooting up, it was a game changer, for sure. The changes in him made it so I would absolutely not ever do this. There was one time when I was very sick and a friend showed up at my house saying she only had what was already loaded in a needle and I begged her to just do it, but fortunately she did not. I am forever grateful I never did this, because I feel like it would have intensified my situation way more than what I even want to think about.

During the worst of my addiction, I was stealing anything I could to get high. I would go get things under a certain price so I could return them with no receipt to get money for a fix. I treated my mother awful, at times telling her I'd rather die than feel like I did and guilt her into giving me money. I lied about what I needed money for. I stole checks and credit cards and anything else I could get. Other addicts would call me to get them drugs, and I would give them fake drugs and keep the real ones. Or I would take half of it, then still make them share with me. I did not have any remorse about any of this, feeling entitled to everything. Now, I have a lot of things to work through, and a lot of work to get back in my family's good graces. I don't know if this is possible, but I will do everything in my power to try.

When people say addicts should "just stop," I still roll my eyes. People do not understand that it feels like you need the drugs to live. Being dope sick is like the worst flu ever, intensified 10 times. You feel like your skin is crawling, you want to rip it right off. You have absolutely no energy. You have goose bumps, but are hot. Or you're sweating, but freezing. You are vomiting and have diarrhea, and are probably already dehydrated so it's even worse. You shake so bad sometimes you can't light a cigarette, not that it matters because even though you want one so bad, the second you taste it, you will probably dry heave and vomit again. There's an awful taste in your mouth and a tickle in your throat that is unbearable. Then there are the restless legs. I went to detox for about a day and a half the first time, and in that amount of time I had restless legs so badly that I wore holes in my ankles all the way to the bone. I still have the scars. It is a feeling that you would literally rather die than go through this.

I was not stupid. I knew drugs are bad; I was a D.A.R.E. role model, for fuck sake. What I didn't realize was that the medication I was given from a doctor was just as bad as anything I could get on the street. And by the time it got to heroin and cocaine I was so broken, I just didn't care. I just needed to feel normal, and that was the only way I knew how to make that happen. This portion of my chapter was written after I re-read what I had previously written. I hope this can offer some insight to a family struggling with an addict, or the addict themselves. I hope to offer some hope to someone somewhere. There is a better way. You do not have to suffer forever, or die a junkie. I know what a hopeless feeling it is. I know the feeling of wanted to disappear, or die. And now, I don't have to live like that anymore.

November 26, 2016

Today is the day! Today is the first day of the rest of my life! I've finally been admitted to a specific inpatient setting for detoxing in the largest city in our state. I have been calling (nearly) every day for 4 weeks, up to 7 times a day. I am here for detox. The last detox I'll ever have to do. I've held off to come here because they offer a suboxone taper as well as other PRN (as needed) meds. I am writing this laying on my bed in detox, waiting for the rest of the admission process to be done, as well as trying to lower my blood pressure a bit. When they just checked it when I first came in, it was 170/98. My norm is about 110/50.

December 3, 2016

I am in the holy fuck homeless shelter. I went through detox. On my second day there, I called the 9 month residential program I was going into after detox and found out that I could go there Monday morning when I was due to discharge from detox. On day 4, the fucker called me, saying someone with "close family ties" works there, so I'm fucked. I wigged. Signed out of detox. Not sure where I figured I'd go but here I am. Market research. Lived experience. That's what I'm telling myself. I'll be a better person because of it. Fuck. This really sucks. It's the day everyone got their checks (Social Security) so everyone is right fucked up, nodding out. Old people here. What the fuck is wrong with society that we let these sick old people live on the streets and in shelters? The country as a whole needs a fucking overhaul. Veterans. These people fought for our fucking lives and sleep in a scuzzy shelter. What the fuck. Oh! This is my first "sober" writing. Only 4 mg suboxone today!

December 21, 2016

Well, I've made it 23 days today. I'm so fucking blessed I can't even stand it. I am with someone who loves me and we are together and doing amazing. I am writing this from the camper in his bed. I'm waiting on the check from "Help Me Recover" to come in to cover the move in costs for my sober house. My life feels so good. I am stupid grateful for all the blessings. The cost to move in was $430. I could have gotten $250, plus $100 from my mom. So I went to ask for help with the $80. Someone from the local drop in recovery center got me $480! He made me cry saying all kinds of stuff about me, like how good I'm doing. I'm so lucky I have the support I do. I did a short (3 day) suboxone taper and it's been all non-medicated since. Finally my body is feeling better. I went 72 hours with no sleep in a row and several single nights without sleep, but it doesn't seem to be an issue now. Thank God. Speaking of God, I'm really trying to figure that business now. I think I am making progress, but we'll see.

January 1, 2017

I don't think I've ever been so excited for a new year! Today is the first New Year's Day I'm not hungover as fuck, hating life. It's actually quite the opposite! I feel very content and calm. I'm missing my kids like crazy, but I have to be okay that I'm doing what's best for them. From afar. All four of us are thriving, which is amazing to see and know. This is going to be a great YEAR! I was in a room with someone who had dope the other day, and had zero interest in having any. My mind has changed so much in only 33 days. I am so grateful for this. I really didn't want to die…even though I was slowing killing myself every day of my life, gambling with my life every single time I scored dope and laid out a line and did it. Yet I did. But I don't live like that anymore. Thank God.

September 22, 2017

Today, it has been 297 days; 7,143 hours; or 428,630 minutes since I last used heroin or cocaine. Today, I don't feel like I need to count the days, hours or minutes anymore. Today, I'd tell you I have about 9 and a half months clean.

Today, I was able to wake up, at about 6:30, get ready for work, show up and do my job. Without drugs.

Today, I get to be present for my children when I make the trip back home for my daughter's football game she is cheering at, and my boys' youth night.

Today, I get to hug my family, and be forever grateful to be alive.

These are all things that 298 days ago I never thought would be possible. Addiction is such a hopeless disease. I used to sit in my room and think of ways I could promote my death without anyone knowing. I thought of shooting an absurd amount of heroin, then driving a car. Then my family would think it was just a car accident, instead of an overdose. I thought of just walking into the woods until my body gave out. I thought of moving and nobody would know, or particularly care, where I'd gone.

Today I know none of these are the answer.

Addiction is such a selfish disease, as is recovery. I have burdened my family with all the issues that come along with addiction, for a very long time, and continued to do so on Tuesday, November 29th, 2016. I had been arrested on October 1st, and my parents took responsibility for my children. I knew I needed help, but did not know where to turn. My addiction was speaking, and it was speaking loud. Telling me how worthless I am. The kids are in a better place. If I am not there, I will no longer be a burden.

Today, I know this is simply not true.

When I got out of jail, my first stop was my dealer's house. I was not concerned with my children or my family, I just simply had to "get right" before I could deal with any of that. I was very physically sick, and needed a fix. From that point, I just kept going. For nearly another two months, I was out on the streets, doing whatever I could to get high. Food, shelter, basic human needs were not a thought in my mind. I had been calling a detox unit off and on, mostly so my mother would see the number on my phone bill and be happy, but not really trying to get help. On November 29th, I called for the first time actually somewhat hoping to get in. It was not a typical situation, where I was out of drugs and money and was desperate to just get through that part. I actually had both those things, something just changed. I got really high, and called at 10:30 a.m. The woman who answered told me to call back in a half hour. I used again, and actually made that second call. They told me to be there by 1:00 p.m. This scared the shit out of me....I did not really want to go to detox. This was just to show my mom I was "trying". I called my mom, explained I could go, but I couldn't get there because it was 45 minutes away and I had no ride, but oh well. I tried. She hung up, called me right back and said my sister would be right there. I immediately got up, walked to the bathroom and flushed the rest of my drugs. I have no idea what prompted me to do this, but I am so glad I did.

I went into the detox unit for four days. A series of events lead me to leave, and have to spend the night in a homeless shelter. Everyone around me was either high or drunk. It was terrifying. That night a woman from the shelter took me under her wing and kept me there until morning. She told me about the local drop in center and a woman we will call Viki. She told me to go there first thing in the morning and meet with her. I figured I had nothing to lose at this point, so I stayed up all night in the scariest situation I have ever been in and walked away, in a city that I did not know, towards, what my online maps was telling me, was the right direction. Viki took me in and saved my life.

Viki owns a sober house for women in the largest city in our state. She also was a peer support person for people in recovery. She knew exactly what moves to make and when to make them. Thankfully, because I was thinking only of getting back home so I could use again.

Viki talked to me for hours; giving me a little bit of hope that things could be different. I connected with another addict while at the recovery center who offered her apartment to me until I could get into a sober house. I really thought these women were insane. I did not think there was any way possible that they were sober AND happy. It was so confusing to me. I was able to stay with the other girl for what ended up being about six weeks before getting into a sober house. I chose not to go to Viki's house because I valued her as such a friend I did not want to risk messing that up by mixing her and money. I still had a complete lack of trust in myself.

On Sunday, Viki picked me up early in the morning for church. I had not been to church in years, felt like absolute shit and did not sleep well, but I got up to go regardless. While in church, I was unable to stay standing for the three songs at the beginning. I had on a tank top, a long sleeve shirt and two sweatshirts. I was shaking, had cold sweats, goosebumps, no temperature regulation, and was so sick to my stomach I could hardly stand it. I kept taking my top hoodie off and putting it back on. Viki looked at me and asked if I was ok, to which I responded "Yeah, just being reminded I'm alive." I have no idea where that answer came from, but it was a huge revelation for me. I could be dead. Really, I should have been dead. But I wasn't, and that's a miracle in and of itself, and such a blessing.

During the service, the pastor had said the devil is a liar. I had written this down on the paper they gave us, and then in big letters above it wrote HEROIN with an arrow to "the devil". So essentially it said HEROIN is the devil, and the devil is a liar. Later in the service, the pastor said to replace the words the devil with whatever it is you struggle with. I lost it. I was crying right there in front of a ton of people, realizing that I had a huge battle ahead of me, but feeling more prepared than ever to fight, and win, this battle. And a psychic change happened, right there in church.

I continued to stay at the apartment for those weeks that felt like they dragged forever. Every morning, I got up, and walked to the recovery center. I would sit there from opening to close, meeting all kinds of people, going to all the 12 step meetings I could. Viki would bring me to other meetings, introducing me to other people in the community. People have strong opinions on different fellowships, but my feeling is you need to do what you need to do to stay clean and sober. Narcotics Anonymous. Alcoholics Anonymous. Cocaine Anonymous. Other types of fellowships. Whatever works for you, all of them, one of them, shouldn't matter. I feel like getting into a 12 step program is a huge make or break aspect of recovery, and life. When I speak at meetings, I always talk about how I'm grateful I am an addict, because the 12 steps are literally a handbook to life in general and being a better human. I wish "normal people" would at least read the 12 steps and apply them to their lives, because if worked, the steps really make a difference in your outlook on life. We all struggle. Life is hard. We can all use all the help we can get. Getting a sponsor to take you through the steps is huge, as well. A sponsor is a support person who will listen to you, in a nonjudgmental way, and give solid advice. These people have been through the steps, and give instructions and help in getting through it. Step-work is not easy, by any stretch, but neither is being a suffering addict, absolutely hopeless and unable to see your way out. Please know, there is a way out.

So I was able to get into a sober house. That lasted about three weeks, until my roommate got high, passed a drug test then got honest with me in the middle of the night. One of the main rules in this house was that if you knew someone got high you had 15 minutes to tell someone else in the house, but I chose to wait until morning. This provided me with a very important lesson. Now, when I meet people and we become friends, I am straight up with the fact that I will not gossip about them, but if I know they are getting high or I think they are going to, I will tell on them. Every single time.

So, I had 15 minutes to get out of the sober house I had worked six weeks to get into. I was terrified that I was going to have to go back to the shelter, as this is the usual outcome. Fortunately, I had been showing willingness to get better and do the next right thing, and Viki had noticed this. She sent a group text to the girls in her house asking if I could stay on the couch until a bed opened (which was scheduled to happen in about a week and a half). This is highly unusual, but all the girls welcomed me into their house. I was overcome with gratitude, unable to thank them all enough. I was able to stay there until the other girl left, and now am sitting on my bed in that sober house writing this, about 6 months later.

Many things have changed for me. I feel like one of the most important things to do in recovery is to surround yourself with people who are doing well, will call you out on your bull shit (and there's plenty), and offer constructive advice when needed. During my time at the recovery center, daily, there was an employee there who I strongly disliked (I try not to say "hate", but I definitely kind of hated him). And he felt the same way about me. One day my sister had brought me some bags from my house, and hidden in them (unbeknownst to her) I found some drug paraphernalia. I was very stressed about this and tried to go to the center to see Viki, but this other guy was the only one there. When I got there and he was able to pull it out of me what my problem was, he simply asked if I got high, Irritated, I answered no, obviously not. Then he asked if I wanted to. Again, no. Then he basically told me to pull my shit together because obviously something was working right. Well, hell. I hate you, but that was real good advice, however unsolicited. From that day on, I've come to think of him as my best friend. Just tonight, he went back to my hometown to watch my daughter cheer, and my boys and nephew participate in youth football night at the varsity game. He is always there for me, even if it is just to tell me to pull it together. I feel like it's very important to find this person in recovery. I have amazing friends now. Friends who don't want or expect anything from me, and I don't want or expect anything from them.

I am currently looking for an apartment with a woman who came into my life exactly when I needed her.

We both struggle with different things, and help each other get through them and work towards being better people in general. Such an important bond.

My family has been absolutely amazing. Please understand, I've done things to these people that warrant them never talking to me again, and I couldn't even be upset. Yet they've supported my kids through this entire journey with no questions asked. Ten months in there are still people who choose not to be part of my life, and I understand that. I have to prove myself and my intentions to them, and that will take time. They may chose not to talk to me again, and I have to be accepting of where they are at. I love and miss them so much it hurts, but I have put myself here and can't do anything other than the next right thing and hope they are able to forgive me, some day. It gets me down sometimes, but I need to have absolute trust in God's plan and realize I have no control over other people's actions, only my reactions to them. Even in sobriety, when I was having difficulty sleeping and in the middle of my fourth step (the one with the most writing, and realizing your character defects, etc.) I was up at about 2 am and thinking of ways to kill myself again. I felt so hopeless again, feeling like I would never get my kids back, how family would never take me back, I would never get a job, I was going to get a big prison bid (I ended up not having to do any prison time), I would never live a normal life, never be happy again. I just wanted it to be over. I prayed so intensely for this feeling to be removed and to get some hope back and fell asleep. I woke in the morning feeling like I needed to do the work and get moving on my recovery if I wanted these things and have not felt like that since. That was at least six months ago.

I have written numerous times about God and praying. Please don't let this turn you away from recovery. The way I explain praying is this: praying is nothing more than turning your thoughts completely conscious and thinking through the things that come into your mind and subconscious. I personally believe there is something bigger than me, and choose to call that God, simply out of convenience. I feel highly connected to Mother Earth, the universe at large and nature in general. I believe in energy, the power of attraction and surrounding yourself with positivity. I did not believe in anything when I was using. I can tell you that I feel significantly different when I pray and meditate throughout the day versus when I don't. I do not "hit my knees" twice a day. I literally talk to my God all day, every day. I swear like a pirate, and continue that even when talking to my God. Your higher power is something highly personal and to be figured out when it's time for you to do so. My first sponsor told me to pray every day, and I explained I didn't have anything to pray to. She literally told me to start my prayers by saying "Hey, Alana's God...." and continue from there. And apparently it worked as a jump off, because I still do this regularly, though I can now talk directly to my God instead of hers.

Another thing I hope you can hear in this part is gratitude. I have heard a million times "a grateful drunk doesn't drink" or "a grateful addict doesn't use" and this is so very true. I was so blessed in coming into this with outrageous gratitude that has not waivered. Every morning, I wake up, go outside, listen to music and think of at least a few of the things I'm grateful for. Everything from my children being happy and safe, to being tired because I am lucky enough to have a job. I'm grateful to wake up every day and not have to try to lie, cheat and steal to feed a horrific drug addiction. I'm grateful to be so close to getting my kids back living with me. For my family. People in the program. Stars, sunsets, sunrises and tides. The people God has placed in my life to help me through this crazy ride of life, and those who have been placed in mine so I can help, which in turn helps me. Whenever other people come to me because they're struggling, the first thing I say is "rapid fire, quick. Top five things you're grateful for right this minute." I've yet to have someone not feel at least a little better after thinking about this. The key to this isn't always thinking about the good things, though that's important. The turn-around making a negative into a positive is key. You're sad? Good. If you were high you wouldn't be able to feel that emotion. Angry? Good. That means you care enough about something to get to that level.

People have felt like I've become used to being on my own. Not having responsibilities. This is about as far from the truth as it could be. I chose to not focus on the negative emotions that would lead me right back out the door to using, because they are so painful. I chose to show people that recovery is possible, if you put in the work needed. If you have the supports you need and love and support you deserve. I am very blessed to be so close to having my children back living with me, I can hardly even wait. That said, I am working very hard to continue doing the work that has gotten me to where I am today. I want a place that's acceptable to me for my boys to live, and my daughter to come to as she wishes. I took these kids into a very dark life, for a very long time. They deserve so much better, and I hope and pray every single day I can make that happen for them. I still feel a lot of self-doubt, guilt, shame. I have to pray (have conscious thoughts) about this because I know with the program and supports I have I can make that happen.

Another critical part of recovery is working. Something as simple as getting a job can make a huge difference in your complete outlook and state of mind. The more recent studies show a 67% increase in success in long term recovery with a job, versus not having a job. We spend all our time and energy getting and using drugs. You have to fill that time. The other side of that is that it does not have to be a high stress job. I am college educated, with numerous state certifications to work in a few fields. I currently clean hotel rooms. I literally make beds and scrub toilets to make a living, and love every second of it. I was able to find a job that's highly supportive of recovery. My boss, has been there for me 100% since day one. I am allowed the days off I need in order to meet my children's needs, and the needs of my recovery. She told me one day that if I relapse, she will find me and hurt me. As a very stern woman, I believe her. And I love that. I asked her one day why she continues to hire addicts, and she very simply said "I think you all deserve a chance. I know you can change, I believe in you." Such a simple statement has stayed with me the whole time I've worked there. And that, and the empty threat of violence, has helped me through some pretty rough times.

When I was using, I literally had no faith or hope in anything. Addiction in such a hopeless place to be. You don't even live there, because you are merely surviving. Sometimes, you are able to put on a nice outfit and smile, but it is all so fake. That said, there are certainly times in sobriety that I "fake it until I make it". Or I am miserable. Life is hard. It takes a lot of work to undo years of destruction caused by your poor decisions, or disease, depending on your view. Addiction is clearly a family situation. It pulls the entire family down, and it can take the entire family to make long term recovery a success. Family does not have to be blood. I am blessed enough to still have blood family that is there for me, whether they can show it right now or not is irrelevant, but also friends who have become family. A few weeks ago in church my pastor said "If you tell me who your five closest people are, I can tell you where you'll be in five years." This is something my father has tried to beat into my head for years, and I simply did not believe it until my five closest people changed, and my entire life changed. Today, I have so much. Today, I can live.

My most intense hope is to be able to share the hope I have for positivity and change. I am not the same person I was ten short months ago. 297 days ago. Even 60 days ago. I am a work in progress, but I really like where this progress is going.

My mom recently told me she finally has her daughter back. I've been so lost for so long, I asked her how she knows and she explained that she hadn't realized how far gone I was, but now that I'm back she can feel it and she knows it. She told me she had forgotten how big my eyes are. That was devastating. I was so high for so long my own mom didn't remember who I am. I feel like I don't even know who I am, but I'm excited to find out. I will be 33 years old in a few weeks, and feel like I missed some serious time, but there is nothing I can do at this point to change that. However, I am looking forward to what the rest of my life holds, and am forever grateful that I still have a life to live. Not everyone is lucky enough to even make it out alive. August 31st is Overdose Awareness Day, and I was involved in an event. That was so difficult. There was a police officer there who was too late to save his daughter when she overdosed in his house. That could have been my father telling our story. The similarities were mind-blowing, and really very difficult to listen to. I don't want to make my father cry anymore. I don't want him waiting for the police to show up to tell him I've either overdosed or done some dumb shit that has gotten me killed. This is a reality my father has had to live with far too long. I don't want my mom to wake up from nightmares of me and my kids not being safe. I don't want to ever have to hear them say "I love you very much, but I hate you right now". Please do not judge them by this, it totally makes sense. I deserved that, and still do sometimes. It is also one of the things that has stuck with me and helped me stay sober through some things I might not otherwise stay sober through.

After the Overdose Awareness event, I was able to talk to the chief of police who has done some amazing things in her town. It takes entire communities to make these things come to life. It is so much work, but if we can stop our kids from becoming another generation of people addicted to these drugs, it is all worth it. Again, I am so grateful to have made it out the other side with my life to witness and be part of this movement.

Today, I am about nine and a half months clean and sober.

Today, I am able to put these words on paper, in a logical order.

Today, I am able to appreciate the beauty of the universe around me.

Today, I hug my niece, and thank her for sharing her love of the stars with me.

Today, I show up for my family, be someone they can be proud of, and be present for them.

Today, I can give and receive pure love for exactly what it is, no strings attached.

Today, I can live.

Today, I am free.

Chapter 9

An Update

Today, as we all approach the last month of 2017, I am writing the last entry to our book. We all think it only right to update everything one more time to ensure some form of completeness to this part of our life journeys. There are still many challenges and difficulties, but things are much better.

Nicole has been one year clean and sober as of yesterday. This is something we are so happy about and most of us are really proud of her and her success. Her peers in recovery must be, too, as all of us were just informed yesterday, that annually her recovery center picks a person to receive a big award (a community donated, completely restored, late model car). They chose Nicole to receive it, for her dedication to her recovery, the support of others in their recovery and her work on the 12 Steps. This unexpected blessing was the final thing needed for her to move into her own place and have the boys back to live with her.

My husband and I still have all three of her children living with us and we are very tired, not of them but just the work. We are getting "old", haha! He and I have continued to have stress in our marriage and at least every few weeks there is a big event that we have to navigate to get back to liking each other. We have never stopped loving, but this again has uncovered some huge stress fractures in our relationship, which I hope we survive. Remember, our goal was never to sugar coat this process, but to be as honest as we could with what we have felt, at any given time. He and Nicole have not talked in one year, almost, and she, not having gotten the boys back yet, has added to the gap. Nicole understands that her amends in this situation are probably going to be the hardest, but she says she will get us all back to being in relationship with each other, not the same one, but a better one. My husband is not so sure.

Our other daughter and our son-in-law have been very successful in staying true to each other and have stayed deeply in love and committed to one another through these 14 months. Our son-in-law has very little tolerance for her stories of what is going on in her life. He sees how difficult it is for us, as well as his own wife, to juggle all of Nicole's responsibilities and is not happy she has not relieved all of us of this stress. They have made it through ups and downs with Nicole and are learning to tolerate, if not openly embrace her, new and improved. They still have future problems they will need to overcome in their relationship with Nicole but they seem very committed to her, too. Their three children have been all love and openness in seeing their 'auntie' again. All is good!!

Our son is in his junior year of college and it is only 80 days to the opening face-off at the first lacrosse game of the season. Through this year he became the first player from his college to make both the all-conference team and the all state lacrosse team. Huge accolades for a boy from a small town community. He has really manage the come-back with Nicole too. After his thanksgiving weekend here at home, he was driving back to school and stopped in the city she lives in to see Nicole and they talked, solidly, for about an hour. Both told me it was so nice to just be together. Keep fingers crossed it continues that way. He is clear, he will never forgive her if his nephews and niece have to suffer again.

Our granddaughter is doing great, academically and socially. She has developed a strong group of real friends who know her history, know she lives with us and do not judge or talk about any of her private issues. She is not alone in having difficulties and some of them want to write in the next book what it is like to be the friend of a daughter whose parents have addictions. Two weeks ago at the Varsity Cheering Awards night, she received the "Most Dedicated" trophy that was voted on by the members of her squad. She was proud and deeply appreciated that they noticed all she puts into being a support for her team. Nicole, her mom was not there.

Finally, the boys have continued to maintain their weight loss and athletic abilities. They are still very proud of their bodies and appreciate all the complements. A. still has problems not being bossy or over talking adults. This is always worse when he comes back from being with the other grandparents, who frequently take the boys to see their dad in prison. Their dad tells A. he is the man of the house and that plays out in some very disruptive ways. We all are working on this with him, but it is very difficult to have to tell the other grandparents and their father to not put all that pressure on an 8 year old. W. just had another significant surgery at the beginning of November, but recovered super from it. Again, Nicole went and was all she needed to be for him as a mother, but she went back to Portland, and I took him to support him through the recovery. He was out of school for 10 days but kept up all his homework and is socially doing well. They are wonderful kids that will always need strong guidance to off-set earlier years.

We are still the family of a heroin addict and we are still making it through every day, together!!!

Again, thanks for all the support and keep up with all of us through our website, blog, and other social media and look for the next book of our trilogy, "We are the Extended "Family" of a Heroin Addict" illustrating the widening circle of what one person's addiction does to those around them.

Family Forever!

Printed in the United States
By Bookmasters